PROSPER...

What Venezuela needs...

Edited by Rafael Acevedo

Prosperity & Liberty:
What Venezuela needs...

Edited by Rafael A. Acevedo R.
Published by Econintech under the Creative Commons Attribution
NonCommercial-NoDerivs 4.0 International License.
http://creativecommons.org/licenses/by-nc-nd/4.0/

ISBN: 9781093507034

Cover designer: Luis Marchena

For more information about this book:

In Venezuela: Asociación Civil Econintech,
Av. Pedro León Torres, Residencias Cristinas, Apto. 303, Barquisimeto,
Edo. Lara, Venezuela, 3001
Teléfono: +58-412-153-5060

In USA: Econintech Inc., Miami Florida. Phone: +1-786-474-0484

Web: www.econintech.org Email: contacto@econintech.org

For more information, conferences, interviews, and lectures about this
book, please contact directly to the editor: rafael.acevedo@econintech.org
and follow him in his Twitter: @RAAcevedoR

Edited & Printed in the USA thanks to the generosity and support of
Econintech's friends, members, partners and donors.

Econintech is a Civil Association registered in Barquisimeto – Lara
State, Venezuela as a non-profit, non-governmental, non-partisan,
organization, RIF: J-40690014-1.

Econintech Inc. is a tax exempt 501(c)(3) non-profit organization
registered in Florida State, USA, contributions are tax-deductible to the
full extent the law allows, Tax ID# 83-3623352.

For all people that still believe and fight for freedom in dangerous places like Venezuela. For those that have to open their eyes to the real results of Socialism, please do not let your country to be destroyed by that system. And, to the next generation of Venezuelans, perhaps, you will have the opportunity, we hadn't, to apply these reforms and allow Venezuela to enter to the real road of Prosperity & Liberty.-

R.A.

ACKNOWLEDGMENT

I want to thank authors for the collaboration and help they gave me in this project, without you this could not be possible. An especial thanks to the Free Market Institute at Texas Tech University and its entire faculty and staff; this book was possible because of the opportunity of having me as a Research Associate. Also, I want to thank Luis Cirocco for his collaboration in the proofreading of some of the essays in the English version, and Luis Marchena for his patience in the design of the covers for the Spanish and English version. To Hugo Faría for his help during the edition of this book. To all of Econintech's team that promotes my work. And, my family that accompanies me in –and back- all my endeavors, you shall always be in my heart. Thanks to God for being ever helping and guiding me in my life. God bless America, the United States, Venezuela, and all people that made possible this project and believe that my country and the world have a real way and hope to the long-run Prosperity & Liberty.-

Rafael Acevedo

CONTENTS

v

EPILOGUE

vi

FOREWORD

Most humans, in most places, throughout most of human history, lived in poverty. Even today, poverty is not unusual. There are still billions of people living in poverty in countries that have never achieved a modern level of economic development. However, it is extremely rare to see a country that had escaped the poverty of the past and achieved a high standard of living for many of its people, rapidly plunge back into poverty. Unfortunately, that is what has happened in Venezuela.

Venezuela was wealthy in the not too distant past. In 1957, Venezuela's Real GDP per capita was half of that in the United States. It was also relatively economically free. The Economic Freedom of the World Annual Report scored Venezuela's economic freedom a 7.2 out of a maximum of 10 in 1970. That made it the 10th freest economy in the world at that time. Unfortunately, 1970 is the first year this index ranking is available. It is likely that Venezuela was even more economically free before its social democratic era began in 1958.

By 1995, three years before Hugo Chávez was elected, Venezuela's economic freedom score had dropped to 4.35 and its ranking had plummeted to 106th. By 1998, incomes averaged only 15 percent of U.S. levels. The social democratic era in Venezuela created a stagnant economy, and the poor were discontent and angry with elite crony capitalists, who benefited from favors bestowed on them by interventionist government officials. Hugo Chávez's promises of the changes his brand of Bolivarian Socialism would bring resonated with voters and he was elected president with 56.2 percent of the popular vote, in what is widely viewed as a fair election.

Chávez's policies began slowly wrecking the already damaged Venezuelan economy. Meanwhile, high oil prices, coupled with the world's largest proven oil reserves, masked the economic carnage from most people's view. When prices (and production because of government mismanagement) came down after Chávez's death, the Venezuelan economy completely collapsed.

Chávez and Nicolás Maduro's socialist policies have landed Venezuela dead last in the economic freedom out of the 162 countries ranked today and left the economy in shambles. Almost 90 percent of Venezuelans now live in extreme poverty. There are shortages of food, medicine and other basic necessities; people are going hungry. Maternal mortality has risen 65 percent and infant mortality 30 percent. But the hardships faced in Venezuela today are not 'typical' 3rd world poverty.

I spent time on the Colombian and Venezuelan border in January of 2017 in the course of doing research for my book, coauthored with Robert Lawson, "*Socialism Sucks: Two Economists Travel the Unfree World*". Venezuelans were free, at that time, to cross back and forth to Colombia across the two bridges over the Río Táchira that connected Cúcuta, Colombia, with Venezuela. They were doing so by the thousands each day, in order to buy food and other basic necessities that were unavailable in Venezuela because of the government policies that had destroyed the incentive and ability of entrepreneurs to meet the demands of consumers.

It was striking to observe that most of the people crossing the border to purchase necessities were middle-class to upper middle-class judging by their clothing, luggage, and, when we spoke with them, their occupations. The truly impoverished Venezuelans lacked the means to make the long journey to the border, or the wealth to purchase much once they got there. But socialist policies had wreaked such havoc that middle class people were now resorting to desperate means to acquire even basic goods.

As noted above, Chavez was democratically elected (and re-elected) to usher in his socialist policies. Venezuela was democratic socialism. As recently as 2011, Bernie Sanders claimed, "These days, the American dream is more apt to be realized in South America, in places such as... Venezuela... where incomes are actually more equal today than they are in the land of Horatio Alger. Who's the banana republic now?"[1]

But as socialist policies wrecked the economy, voters lost their ability to dispose the regime impoverishing them. For much of 2017, Chávez's successor, Nicolás Maduro, had an approval rating that hovered between 20 and 30 percent, and anti-government protests abounded. Yet he was re-elected by a wide margin, in an election that everyone knows was a fraud.

In his 1944 book, The Road to Serfdom, Friedrich Hayek argued that a competitive capitalist economy is necessary to sustain democracy, and that once a country becomes "dominated by a collectivist creed, democracy will inevitably destroy itself."[2] The reason is simple. Centrally planned, socialist economic systems necessarily concentrate economic power in the hands of government planners who can, through their economic edicts, punish dissent. This is exactly what has happened in Venezuela. Democratic socialism evolved into mere socialism.

At a time when 'democratic' socialism is enjoying increased popularity in the United States, these two lessons are important for the readers of the English language edition of this book. Venezuela was democratic and relatively rich when it was economically free. The situation they find themselves in today is not 'normal' third world poverty nor does it have anything uniquely Latin American about it. Their loss of meaningful democratic freedom and poverty are both a necessary consequence of their adoption of socialist economic policies. Despite socialist U.S. politicians' claims to favor democracy, we can expect a similar journey down the Road to Serfdom in the United States if we adopt socialist economic policies.

---

[1] Valley News Editorial Board, "Close The Gaps: Disparities That Threaten America," August 5, 2011, available at:
https://www.sanders.senate.gov
[2] Friedrich Hayek, The Road to Serfdom (Chicago: University of Chicago Press, 1944), 69-70.

Although U.S. readers will benefit from the lessons contained in Prosperity & Liberty: What Venezuela Needs, the primary value of this book is the lessons and recommendations it contains for Venezuelans going forward.

As I write this foreword in March 2019, there is a political struggle for control of the Venezuelan government. Juan Guaido has been named interim President by the national assembly and recognized as the legitimate head of state by the United States and most European and Latin American countries. Yet, through the military, Maduro hangs on to power.

Maduro and his socialist policies have to go if Venezuela is to prosper again. However, as Rafael Acevedo and I argue in this book's post-script, the problem is that Guaido is a socialist too. Guaido and his allies are more united in their opposition to Maduro's leadership than to the failed socialist policies. They want a return to democracy, but with the same big government meddling of the economy that pre-dates Chavez.

Guaido's policies will not turn Venezuela's economy around. Instead, Venezuela needs to make radical reform that embrace free markets. Many of the chapters in Prosperity & Liberty: What Venezuela Needs, provide the guidebook for the needed reforms. Some chapters have detailed explanations of the precise policy reforms needed in Venezuela. Equally importantly, other chapters illustrate examples of how other countries have radically reformed by embracing free markets and the economic success that has accompanied the reforms.

In this regard, I think Chapter 9, by Larisa Burakova and Robert Lawson, is particularly important. In a little over a decade the Republic of Georgia transformed itself from a corrupt post-Soviet economy into one of the 10 freest economies in the world. Following the 2004 Rose Revolution, a reformist government fired bureaucrats, privatized state assets, ended corruption, and slashed taxes. In response, the country has been growing rapidly. Some of the particulars of Venezuela's situation differ, of course, but both the challenges and opportunity are similar to those that

Georgia confronted.

Ultimately, reform in Venezuela needs to come from Venezuelans demanding change and holding their government accountable for making those changes. The United States, World Bank, IMF, or any other outsider cannot force the type of institutional reform that is necessary. Ideas that captivate the hearts and minds of citizens are ultimately what can create and enforce the needed reforms. Prosperity & Liberty: What Venezuela Needs has exactly the type of ideas in it that are necessary. I hope that they will captivate the minds of Venezuelans and help to get the country off the road to serfdom and back on the path to prosperity.

Benjamin Powell
Lubbock, Texas
March 2019.

PROLOGUE

FUNDAMENTAL PRINCIPLES OF A REAL PROPOSAL FOR LIBERTY[3]

When I decided to work and edit this book, I wanted to offer to the public, not only the Venezuelan, a general idea of the current situation in my country and its main cause, Socialism. I also wanted to show that there are people who have dedicated their work to analyze and propose solutions far different from the most announced - Keynesian and Socialist plans - although unfortunately, it is highly probable that one of the latter will be applied after the Venezuelans overthrown the narco-tyranny. Therefore, this book could be a proof, in the not too distant future, that there were other proposals, which really ensured long-run prosperity and freedom. I wanted, as a prologue, to include this article were I explain my views about what are the fundamental principles that a program of liberty should have. This is a summary of an article published in two parts on the blog in Spanish of The Independent Institute. Finally, I hope you enjoy reading this book as much as, or much more than, I enjoyed editing it.

Venezuelan society should understand the importance of analyzing projects that some people promote. The comprehension of causes and selection of strategies to overcome the current disaster is required to succeed. Understanding what real freedom is and open the way to young people, still not corrupted by the socialism and mercantilism, is also needed so that Venezuela can get out of the misery that the pre and post-Chávez era inflicted it.

---

[3] I thank Jeff Diest, President of the Mises Institute, for his suggestions, comments and opinion on this prologue.

Perhaps, all people that promote their own proposals do this with some "good intention." Nonetheless, that does not mean that such a proposal is the best option for the individual. I would not like you understand this prologue such as an inquisitor or a "finger" signaling and condemning people or groups because of their proposals. Common people have to identify who are the fake promoters of liberty and which is the best Project to real freedom. Somebody said once: Countries have the government they deserve... in our case, Venezuelans will have the country – after the tyranny is overthrown- that they choose.

In this prologue, I only give my opinion and suggestions because I prefer the reader himself can understand if a project proposed to overcome the crisis, not only in Venezuela, really promotes true freedom to the citizen. The fundamental thing is analyzing the proposal and be sure that it has principles of liberty, that -per Palmer (2013)- are the following:

> *) **Individual Rights:** individuals have rights that are prior of the political association ...
> *) **Spontaneous Order:** ...the most important kinds of order in society are not the results of conscious planning or design, but emerge from the voluntary interaction and mutual adjustments of plans of free persons acting on the basis of their rights.
> *) **Constitutionally Limited Government:** rights require protection by institutions that are empowered to use force in their defense, but... they must be strictly limited through constitutional mechanisms... (Pp: 31 – 32)

Therefore, if you want to restore economic order and overcome poverty in Venezuela, or in any country, you must prioritize individual rights before anything else. These rights are Freedom, Private Property and Life, also known as Natural Rights or God giving Rights. I always say that there are eight elements that any program that really ensures freedom must have. I summarize them here, and whoever wants to read them

xiii

in more detail I invite him to read my article published –in two parts- on the Spanish blog of The Independent Institute.

1. *Freedom is inherent to the individual NO the State*

When there is a State that enjoys full freedom, we will have aberrations as before Chávez with the group of "notables," deciding the course and destiny of the rest of society, or after Chávez with "the cartel of the suns." Therefore, the State - Government- can not have the capacity –liberty- to decide on such important aspects as, among others, devaluation, legal tender, international transactions, establish or increase a tax before that the society approves it, because simply these "attributions" are the 'most legal way' for a state to steal its citizens.

2. *All State ownership comes at the expense of individual rights*

In other words, the state cannot "own" anything not first produced or paid for by individuals. The state itself produces nothing. For this reason, keep the control – administration- and state ownership of any enterprise - even if they call it "strategic" – is an unquestionable assassination of an individual right of its citizens and gives to the State great power and independence – giving it the freedom I previously mentioned it cannot have -.

3. *The State exists to serve individuals, not the other way around*

The State is an entity that has been created by society to serve it and perform functions that at the time of its creation, for technological reasons or convenience, cannot be executed directly by individuals. This same entity has always ended up being a danger against the freedom of those who created it. The only ones who have the right to life are the individuals and, I would like to remark –in my personal opinion- that even though this right is inalienable, it is possible to think about capital punishment for persons, but this is another debate that deviates from the primary objective of this book.

4. The State can be altered or abolished; it's perpetuation is not guaranteed

As the State has no right to life, it has to be subject to the "capital punishment." In other words, any proposal should include the possibility to get rid of the State of essential functions when the private sector can do those functions, as well as add the possibility of secession.

5. Incentives Matter

A project of freedom must promote right incentives so that nobody –or a least a minimum part of the population- want to be part of the Government. Being a true entrepreneur –not a crony-should be more profitable instead of being a "politician." It is important to create incentives to eliminate a permanent and lucrative bureaucratic class but encourage a dynamic entrepreneurial class.

6. No central planning!

There can not be a superior entity that orders or plans what must be done to "work well." This is the great error of the "Central Planners," their vision of the economy as a whole, where they can plan at the whim of the "wise and disciplined" policymaker, for example, to reach an utopian "full employment."

7. Voluntary and spontaneous transactions play a leading role in freedom

That is why the State can not intervene in voluntary and spontaneous transactions among individuals. Notwithstanding, and because the State has no right to life, any proposal must include possibilities of voluntary associations, which means that individuals can assume a role that the State is not executing correctly or does not reach the society's expectations. It is required to understand –and respect- that each person is an agent capable of creating independent and voluntary relationships, and solving problems, with their peers to achieve their objectives. As well as know that society will always align efforts to achieve objectives and impose a natural and "spontaneous order" long before a bureaucratic apparatus appears and obstructs what could naturally flow and be more successful.

8. The State must be limited, both constitutionally and through the principle of subsidiarity

The only way to ensure that the State does not attempt against the citizen is to limit it as much as possible. We do nothing by writing articles, books, proposals, giving lectures, explaining, debating (sometimes fighting), if at the end of the day the State is not limited. This is only achieved through the constitutional route. You have to write a new constitution that establishes the limits of the State only, for the moment, the monopoly of violence and justice and has to be adjusted to the English *Common Law*. The new constitution should have escape valves in a system (like the Swiss) of complete subsidiarity and easily-met requirements for public referenda in order to eliminate a possible increment in the size of the State.

Final Remarks

I always say that once the tyranny is overthrown, anything anybody does will have a rebound effect in the economy. Many central planners, which is almost a fact that unfortunately, we will fall into their hands, will say that it is the "New Economic Miracle" thanks to its planning. However, that will be an instant recovery that if we do not take advantage of establishing real freedom, we will return, long before these planners die, to misery, and of course, as good socialists will have someone to blame. That is why I emphasize the need to analyze the proposals presented to you by your politicians.

The new Venezuela must be a real country of freedom to which many of those who have emigrated can and, above all, want to return. The latter will be possible if they are sure that their return will not be the beginning of the history of misery and subsequent escape of their children or grandchildren, repeating what many of us had to suffer, but it is really a return to work, live, enjoy and rest in a country that has the fundamental principles of a real long-run prosperity and freedom.

Rafael Acevedo
Lubbock, TX
March, 2019

INTRODUCTION[4]

How was it possible for a country like Venezuela, with an abundance of natural resources, a relatively small population, of 30 million people, and the potential to be the Hong Kong, New Zealand, Poland, or Georgia, of Latin America, to end being in the most miserable country of the world?

This question is raised wherever I make a presentation about Venezuela. And, the answer is straightforward: it was possible because Socialism (Social-Democracy) was implemented in 1958 and then changed to a much harsher form of tyrannical Socialism (Socialism of XXI century) in 1998. Even with this long period of dominance, however, many Venezuelans still do not understand the real meaning of this system, and have not learned that the current misery is a result of policies that re-distribute and destroy wealth. In fact, many Venezuelans still believe that these policies are desirable.

When I left Venezuela, I promised myself that I would continue working for freedom in my country. Wherever I am Venezuela will be my country, but I changes things have to be made before I can return. The people of Venezuela must understand the tremendous benefits of true freedom and terrible costs they are bearing because of socialism. Regrettably, since I left, the misery created by the country's narco-tyranny continues unabated.

A considerable portion of my fellow citizens still seem to worship individuals in power and not examine the projects and ideas they are promoting. This has been a characteristic of Venezuela's population for a long time. People continue to admire past Messiahs and wait for a new one who will end their

---

[4] I thank Professor Bruce Benson, emeritus from the Department of Economics in Florida State University, for his suggestions and comments on this introduction.

1

misery through more socialism. As I am writing this introduction, Venezuelans are posting a picture of Guaidó on social media, and declaring that he is the president that Venezuela deserves because the photo shows him eating "empanadas" and drinking "papelón con limón" in a flea market. Many of my fellow citizens have not learned from the past, and are repeating what others did with Chávez, Caldera, Carlos Andrés Pérez, Lusinchi, Luis Herrera, Leoni, and Betancourt.

As I observe what is happening in Venezuela, my colleagues and I have been working on several Econintech's proposals to solve, once and for all, the crisis and reduce the misery people are suffering there. For this, we focus on two crucial tasks. First, we hope to educate people about the importance of economic freedom as the best trigger to achieve growth and development through entrepreneurship, investment, innovation, and technology. Second, we are proposing a real pro-free-market plan to rebuild not only Venezuela but also any country devastated by tyranny and socialism.

Our plan is to protect natural rights, which means taking special privileges away from the government and the elites it favors. For example, we propose to eliminate the monopoly of the currency, exclude protectionist policies for political cronies, eliminate the minimum wage and encourage flexibility in the labor market, privatization of all state-owned enterprises and assets, and so on. An enormous problem has been created by the combined effects of a wide array of bad policy decisions. Elites in government and who benefit from government favoritism will despise our reforms. Politicians want to keep control of monetary and fiscal policies; otherwise, they will not have their favorite populist weapons to enslave people. Cronies, the economic elite, will never agree that a real free economy should be implemented in Venezuela. This is probably their worst nightmare; they would have to compete in a free and open international trade rather that enjoy the monopoly power the government has given them. Social Media in Venezuela is dominated by Socialists who will never support a proposal such as ours because their power to influence people would be undermined as Venezuelans begin to observe and then understand the tremendous gains that can arise in a free market.

I usually exemplify Venezuela's situation with a medical example. Changing the kind of socialism (Chavismo for MUD or some other variety) is like trying to cure lung cancer by changing the brand of cigarettes the lung-cancer victim smokes. The only real possibility for a cure requites the to stop smoking all brands. Venezuela has a cancer caused by socialism. It cannot be cured by another brand of socialism. It must stop taking the socialist carcinogen.

In light of this metaphor, I divided the core of the book into three parts; the first is the "Symptoms and Causes" where the origins and carcinogen culprits of our misery are examined. The second, "Successful Cures", examines four countries that successfully cured the kind of socialist cancer that Venezuela suffers from, and today they are on the road to recovery: prosperity and economic liberty thanks to the real free-market reforms. In the third part, the "General Treatment," the cure will be described with discussion of, the most updated proposals to eradicate the misery and get rid of socialism. Finally, as an epilogue, I present an OpEd that Benjamin Powell and I wrote about what Venezuela needs.

This book contains a series of essays by well-recognized American professors such as Walter Block, a leading Austrian economist, and Steve Hanke who is always willing to collaborate with us in the fight for freedom in Venezuela. In addition, contributions from Robert Lawson, whose work has ever been a reference in Econintech conferences where, including the Economic Freedom of the World Index, and Benjamin Powell, Director of the Free Market Institute and eminent pro free-market scholar.

When I talked about this project to the Atlas Network CEO, Brad Lips, he suggested that I contact Professor Leszek Balcerowicz from Poland, who sent me one of his articles and gave me permission to create a short version and include it. The

Montreal Economic Institute, who hold the rights of Jean Minardi's papers, kindly authorized inclusion of his economic note on Hong Kong.

As I had the permits of Robert Lawson and the Antigua Forum of Universidad Francisco Marroquin to publish a short version of one of the chapters of his book, I did not contact Larisa Burakova -the other author- nevertheless, I also thank her. Dan Mitchell was a great advisor during the process of this project, suggested examples of successful countries that applied free-market reforms. Alejandro Chafuén, who I had meet in my Smith Fellowship in Atlas Network in 2017, immediately accepted my invitation to write an article for this book.

Last, but not least, I can always count on my Econintech's team, María Lorca-Susino, Hugo Faría, Luis Cirocco, Luis Marchena, and Humberto Andrade, I have for help with all my projects, as we continue working together to create hope of prosperity & liberty. Our work is focused on solving the problems that Venezuela, as well as any country in the same situation, has. We intent to promote real freedom, and hope that someday real pro free-market government can apply these reforms wherever they are needed.

Readers can choose what essay read first, as the order does not really matter. Nevertheless, I hope that they will read the whole book, as it provides a general overview of the causes and cures for the horrible situation Venezuelans are suffering under.

This book does not cover all the reforms we promote through Econintech's activities. However, it is intended to inform the general public, so it does not contain complex mathematical modelling, or econometrics, even though I, and the majority of my collaborators, use these tools in our academic research to establish rigorous proofs and evidence supporting our proposals. That level of sophistication is not required to understand the best way to prosper.

An example of other reforms not discussed in detail in this

4

volume but that Venezuela needs is change in political institutions. One beneficial change would be to from the presidential form of government for a collegial government - such as Switzerland-, I have been working on this subject but I could not finish it for inclusion in this book. The tyranny put my coauthor, Lieutenant-Colonel Rafael Díaz Cuello, in jail. He has been in prison since October 2018, just days before he was going lecture in an Econintech conference. Sadly, anonymous sources report that he has suffered from torture, as he does not belong to any socialist party nobody has been able to talk about him.

Other reforms are also required in the social area. We have to change the belief that a society must be maintained by the government to recognize that a good government must be supported by the society. We need to change the reality of a large portion of the citizens working for a giant and omnipotent state to a new reality in which citizens can be entrepreneurial and employ other citizens, while a small state works for and is controlled by the citizens. We have to shift the reality of a society enslaved by the government through populism for a society that allows free-market forces to overcome poverty.

I will be happy if this book opens the eyes of Venezuela's gullible people, central planning economists, and politicians who believe in, and promote socialism in any of its varieties. They must recognize that this is not a road to recovery for Venezuela or any other country. Also, I will be very pleased if young people read the book and understand that opening the door to socialism is like letting an assassin and rapist get into your home.

Soon I will publish a book that explains all needed reforms in political, economic and social structures. My friend, Humberto Rivero, always says, "Rafael you have to publish the book of Econintech's reforms, as the Chicago's Boys did in Chile, but ours will be close to the Austrian School." My team recognize that the Chicago-Chilean experiment –despite its success- failed to recognize the important implications of the Austrian School of economics. Humberto is right, and my team will finish the complete work in order to publish our own "El Ladrillo".

5

Econintech is not a large International Center, with millions in donations. We are a small think tank with a small and tight budget. My team has their own duties and responsibilities; they work in Universities, the private sector, and as entrepreneurs developing new projects. As a result, we lack the resources that would allow us to work faster and gain more publicity. We fight for freedom for Venezuela and the world.

Finally, I assure the young people who are fighting, like the Movimiento Libertad Venezuela and others, that as they win the political battle, we will continue working on providing them with information about what can be done to put Venezuela on a true long-run road to Prosperity & Liberty.

Rafael Acevedo
Lubbock, TX
March 25th 2019

6

PART 1: CAUSES & SYMPTOMS

1. HOW TO PROMOTE PROSPERITY IN VENEZUELA

By Walter E. Block

Block, with his characteristic wisdom, analyzes some causes of the current Venezuela's disaster. He explains why politicians are in grave error when say that countries such as Norway, Sweden, Finland and Denmark are examples of good socialism and why they avoid discussing Venezuela. Block actually met and shook hands with both Mises and Hayek (he had many discussions with the latter and even played chess with him). Block was mentored by Rothbard and advised in his PhD thesis by Gary Becker. He has had more than 500 articles published in peer reviewed journals and more than two dozen books. Walter Block is the Harold E. Wirth Eminent Scholar Endowed Chair and Professor of Economics at Loyola University in New Orleans, and one of the most recognized and important Austrian Economists of the United States.

Before we offer a way out of the economic thicket in which Venezuela now finds itself in (circa 2018), let us first document its decline. Perhaps from this historical pattern, we may discern a way out of its present morass.

In 1995, Venezuela was the 64th freest country, economically speaking out of 101 counties surveyed. Not very good, but not awful either. But then, in 2010, the ranking in terms of economic freedom for this country fell to 138th out of 141 countries, awful, and in 2015, to dead last, 159th out of 159 countries. It would be impossible to do any worse than that. To illustrate the depths to which this South American country had plunged, the nations ranked just above it, in places 155 through 159, were, respectively, Argentina, Algeria, Congo, and Central African

7

Republic, none of them exactly bastions of economic freedom, and all of them ranked above Venezuela.

Needless to say, but it needs to be said in any case, with this plunge in the ability to engage in commercial interaction, Venezuela's prosperity sunk like a stone. We need not go into depth in this sorry tale. Citizens of this country were not much allowed to vote out of office the perpetrators of this debacle, Hugo Chávez and Nicolás Maduro, so instead they voted with their feet, emigrating to neighboring countries in the tens of thousands. How to calculate the loss of income due to their socialist policies? Statistics are unreliable. But we can see this in the lack of availability in this country of everything from meat to vegetables to diapers to toilet paper. Recently, Hurricane Florence wreaked havoc in North Carolina. The people there were intent on saving stranded dogs. In Venezuela, in sharp contrast, there are reports of starving people actually eating these pets.

We mentioned, above, "socialist policy." This is only an approximation. Yes, there were widespread nationalizations of industry, central planning, heavy regulation of commerce. But even the Soviet Union lasted longer than the time when Chavez began his depredations to the present, when Venezuela for all intents and purposes has fallen apart. Add to the mix vast amounts of sheer theft, and the explanation becomes more clear.

It is of great interest that advocates of socialism in the United States such as Senator Bernie Sanders of Vermont never point to Venezuela as examples of the economic system they would like to see put in place. Instead, the point to the Scandinavian countries such as Norway, Sweden, Finland and Denmark as exemplars of socialism. In this they are in grave error. In order to see this, consider the rankings of these nations in the economic freedom index. Here are the rankings:

1995: Denmark, 33rd place, Finland, 46th, Norway, 41st and Sweden, 48th.

2010: Denmark, 14th place, Finland, 19th, Norway, 31st and Sweden, 37th.

2015: Denmark, 15th place, Finland, tied for 17th, Norway, 25th and Sweden, 27th.

In 1995, there were 101 countries surveyed; these four all ranked in the top half. In 2010, the ratings were calculated for 141 nations; thus all of the Scandinavians made it to the top third. The total number in 2015 was 159; the worst of these countries took 27th place, all of them safely ensconced in the top quartile.

Thus, the claims of Senator Sanders can almost be interpreted as an insult to the people of Venezuela. The latter country is suffering from real socialism, of a gangster variety. Those in the other nations are doing quite well, thank you, based on their residences of among the most capitalist economic systems on the planet. Further, Sweden et al are rich not because of the socialistic income transfers they have recently initiated, but in spite of them. Their wealth stems from the fact that before this welfare system came about, they grew rich due to capitalism.

Venezuela's massive system of price controls led to shortages. This is why basic goods such as toilet paper, baby diapers, became scarcer than hen's teeth in this benighted country. It would appear that this government, under Chávez and Maduro, have never benefited from an elementary course in economics.

For those who do not believe Venezuela has turned into a socialist country, Niño (2018) offers ten reasons:

"1. Abolition of Property in Land and Application of all Rents of Land to Public Purpose.

2. A Heavy Progressive or Graduated Income Tax.

3. Abolition of All Rights of Inheritance.

4. Confiscation of the Property of All Emigrants and Rebels.

5. Centralization of Credit in the Hands of the State, by Means of a National Bank with State Capital and an Exclusive Monopoly.

6. Centralization of the Means of Communication and Transport in the Hands of the State.

7. Extension of Factories and Instruments of Production Owned by the State.

8. Equal Liability of All to Labor. Establishment of Industrial Armies, Especially for Agriculture.

9. Combination of Agriculture with Manufacturing Industries; Gradual Abolition of the Distinction Between Town and Country by a More Equable Distribution of the Population over the Country.

10. Free Education for All Children in Public Schools."

This latter might not sound particularly socialist. Many non-socialist countries have adopted this policy. However, Niño (2018) explains:

"Compulsory education was established by decree in 1880. Public schools in Venezuela now function as indoctrination centers, where millions of youth read the works of Communist figures like Ché Guevara and Fidel Castro in order to 'cleanse' themselves of capitalist thought."

At one time in South American economic history, Chile was a relatively poor country, and Venezuela, thanks to its oil riches and minimal statism, a rich one. Mitchell (2018) accounts for the reversal in this ranking based on economic policies; the former embraced at least a modicum of capitalism, while the latter moved in exactly the opposite direction.

To add insult to injury, Maduro and his ilk have been living high off the hog, while the Venezuelan citizens over whom they rule have been on short rations, near starvation. Bishop (2018) reports Maduro dining on fine steaks while smoking expensive cigars. Nor is this an anomaly. The dictator of Venezuela is not the first socialist to "eat cake" while hapless citizens had their lives ruined.

Let us conclude with McMaken's (2017) question: "Why the Left Refuses to Talk About Venezuela." Which leftists so decline? High up on anyone's list would be almost US president Bernie Sanders and Pope Francis. Both wax eloquent about poverty, income divergences the plight of the "least, last and lost" amongst us. But both have been exceedingly quiet about the chaos now suffering by Venezuelans. Why? It is obvious. It is due to the fact that this country is following, roughly, the economic plans espoused by these two leftists. The chickens are coming home to roost, and Sanders and Francis do not much like the results. Better to focus on the Scandinavian countries.

2. CENTRALIZE EVERYTHING: THE DAWN OF DESTRUCTION

By Rafael Acevedo & Humberto Andrade

Andrade is a journalist that admires Rothbard, Mises, Hayek, and other Austrian Economists. He was a great promoter of the libertarian ideals, but as many Venezuelans, he had to leave the country in his finding for security and a better quality of life for his family. I am honored to having him as the Chief Editor of Econintech. We wrote an article titled "The Death of Venezuelan Federalism –and the Rise of Socialism" published by the Mises Institute in his blog. This article is based upon that published in Mises. I think it is imperative that the world knows the "spark" that gave life to the current disaster. As Block says in his article, before we propose something for Venezuela, we have to really know and understand the culprits of the situation. And the politician and mainstream economist's desire to centralize everything is one of them.

The history of Venezuela is a predicament of centralization. The real curse that our country has is not the "resources curse" or "Dutch disease" but the "politicians curse", because politicians with power, and with possibilities to achieve the power, are a bunch of socialists or cronies. At the moment we are rewriting this article for the book "Prosperity and Liberty: What Venezuela needs", it seems to be that Venezuela still suffers from this curse, there is not a real pro-free-market politician, all of them are related with central planning economists.

The most publicized economic plan of the opposition, rely on an exponential increment of the external debt through institutions with recognized cultural Marxist agendas, and the "great idea" is to recover all state-owned companies, keep the ownership in "strategic enterprises" (such as PDVSA) and the

12

governmental monopoly of money, subsidies the national producers, maintain the "bureaucracy", and "incentive the economy" with an exponential increment in the public expenditure, and more Keynesian strategies. But, let us talk you a little about Venezuela's history.

Despite this could sound ironically, socialism has achieved many times its goal, so it has succeeded. If we analyze the socialistic agenda that politicians started to apply in Venezuela since 1958, it is easy to understand the misery that today Venezuelans suffer and know that is not the failure but the very end stage and success of this system. Indeed, this agenda is the main culprit of why Venezuela with the largest certified oil reserves of the world, the 8th reserves of natural gas, more than 20% of the reserves of the world of Thorium, with Uranium, Copper, Coltan, Bauxite, Gold, fresh water, Silver, in a nutshell, a worth in natural resources of more than US$15 Trillion, and a long history of cultural, political and economic proximity with the United States, ended up being ruled by a narco-terrorist and totalitarian regime that inflicts misery and suffering in people.

Venezuela has had twenty-seven constitutions between 1811 and 1999. Juan Germán Roscio and Cristóbal Mendoza wrote the 1811 constitution, proclaiming the first Republic inspired in the US constitution and the politic liberalism of that moment. The United States of Venezuela was a Federalist government, but it did last just a couple of months when Miranda did capitulate in San Mateo. Nevertheless, the fundamental root of the liberalism and federalism was highly criticized even for many heroes of independence. Bolívar in Cartagena once said referring the 1811 constituents "these gentlemen believe they are in Greece, building air republics that are not consistent with the situation and reality of the Venezuelan people, not prepared for the supreme good of freedom."

Each constitution was made to satisfy the desires and needs of the "caudillo" that ruled the country. Some experts in constitutionalism say that the most federalist was the 1864 Constitution, which expressed a high form of regionalism and

13

localism. Juan Crisóstomo Falcón member of the liberal party of that moment ruled "The United States of Venezuela" -in 1864- but some years after the dictator Antonio Guzmán Blanco counteracted the federalism with the 1881 Constitution. After that, the federalism was increased and decreased depending on the interests of the government.

In 1961 when the 26th Constitution was written by the most recognized socialists of Venezuela -Rómulo Betancourt, Rafael Caldera, Jóvito Villalba, and others- the federalism had been practically eradicated, they ensured some political freedoms and a democratic system, but the economic freedoms were diminished almost to nothing.

Nonetheless, Venezuela seemed in the 1990s aimed to become a federal country. A process called "decentralization" began; it transferred sovereignty and power to each governor of the state; for the first time in the Venezuela history, the people directly elected the state governors through free elections - December 3rd 1989-. It was a humble attempt to redistribute the total control and power that presidents have held, but the main reason was to calm the social situation that worsens after the "Caracazo."

When people elected Hugo Chávez as president in 1998, this third-rate military had promised -among other promises- a new and "better" constitution. The new constitution eradicated the possibility of a decentralization process and, worst of all, increased the size of the State and highly concentrate the power in the president. Allan Brewer Carías analyzes the 27th Constitution of Venezuela, the 1999 or Chavista Constitution, even though he participated in the assembly that wrote it, he did not vote in favor and criticized it because "an opportunity to improve Venezuela was missed" just to give more power to the president.

However, this move toward more executive power will not shock Americans, who are familiar with this trend. We have seen much of it in the US during recent presidential administrations -

14

especially with the War on Terror. Although this is a trend, as Tom Woods tells us, that goes back more than a century.

Therefore, Americans should be careful about a thing that is common in countries where socialism succeeded. The governors' wants and need for more power, the lie "give me more power to give you more free things..." People -especially Millenials- have to remember this quote attributed to President Thomas Jefferson "A government big enough to give you everything you want, is a government big enough to take away everything that you have" and we can put our hands on the fire to testify that is true.

It is essential to recall Javier Pérez-Cepeda's words "In each generation, there is a select group of idiots that think the collectivism failed because they did not rule it." This thought is an excellent description of how socialists think; they will never understand or admit that the only result, or the real success, of that system, is the destruction and misery of the economy and the slavery of the society.

When their system fails socialists that are not ruling the country never say "socialism does not work." On the contrary, they always say "they [the current socialists ruling the country] do not know how to succeed, they were doing wrong things, or this is not socialism" and socialists that are ruling say "we have an enemy sabotaging us [and in Latin America -believe it or not- their enemy is the US]". Considering this, socialists -ruling or not the country- live all their lives trying to increase the size and power of the state. Actually, this is another critical thing to them, the total control and centralization of power. A big and powerful State able to own and manage all the means of production.

Finally, we estimate that despite the new administration in Venezuela will be socialist, the economy will improve in the very short run. Rafael uses to say that any "thing" -he does not use the lousy word-, is better than Chávez and Maduro, nonetheless, the possibility that the economic bounce and prosperity will last forever depend upon the closeness of the

15

rebuilding plan to the real free-market reforms. Sadly, we see that the project more susceptible to be applied is far -ok, less far than the Bolivarian Revolution but still far- from a real pro-free-market program, and on the other hand it seems to promote and keep the centralization and state ownership of the commanding heights of the economy. But as we stated before, this is not new in Venezuela, our history is a predicament of the centralization of power.

3. THE GENESIS OF EVIL

Luis Cirocco is one of the Founder-Directors of Econintech. He is an instructor in Universidad Centroccidental Lisandro Alvarado at the School of Science and Technology. He has a wide experience in the Telecom private sector and is one of the wiser minds, restless and braver figures of Libertarianism in Venezuela. He coined the phrase "The Genesis of Evil" in this article. Luis explains how the Venezuelans elites have a great responsibility to the current disaster in Venezuela. Venezuela should be one of the freest and wealthy countries of the world if free-market oriented policies would have been implemented but the dark interests of those inefficient entrepreneurs and corrupted politicians have played against the Venezuelans' natural rights. Now, Venezuelans have the great challenge of their lives, they should hear the voices of freedom, follow the ideals of liberty, change the nature of policies implemented in Venezuela, which mean open the doors to a new generation of libertarian politicians, and will never ever allow socialism -in any of its varieties- to take the control of the state again, otherwise, "The Genesis of the Evil" will continue killing the burgeoning hope of liberty.

The economy of many European absolute monarchies, during the 16th, 17th and first half of the 18th centuries, centered on a system of monopoly concessions, monetary control, export subsidy, import prohibitions, heavy tax burden, and control of natural resources. The ultimate objective of such system, referred to as mercantilism, was the accumulation of wealth – in the form of gold – by the crown. Nowadays, with the exception that gold is not money anymore and that monarchies were replaced by other forms of government (in some despicable cases, with almost absolute power as well),

17

most of the mentioned vices survive[5].

The most prominent commonality of the mercantilist practices, both past and present, is a high concentration of power in the state. In fact, a large government size[6] introduces high propensity to the emergence of mercantilist activities. Economic elites, integrated, in essence, by inefficient entrepreneurs, lobby bureaucrats to secure privileges. Bureaucrats, in turn, use these relationships to support political projects or increase their own equity. The formal rules of the economic and political game are adjusted to favor these two elitist groups.

In a nutshell, the promotion of a free-market based economy and a less socialist culture hinders the development of unethical practices such as those of past centuries. Then, it is possible to state that there exists sort of a symbiosis between mercantilism and socialism. This relationship of mutual benefit between elites has progressively devastated Venezuela in the last six decades, and has plunged the country into the most severe economic, social and moral crisis of its recent history.

I have called this symbiosis "the genesis of evil", I state that it is the major cause of poverty, exclusion, corruption, indoctrination and other serious problems for the citizens.

The economic disaster in Venezuela did not start with the Chávez-Maduro's regime, but some decades before. Faría and Filardo (2015), with accuracy, describe the progressive institutional deterioration, and contrast the successful results the country exhibited during its decades of greater economic liberalism with those exhibited in the era of the social democracy

---

[5] Above all in the United States of America, *crony capitalism* is the combination of terms used to describe the mercantilist practices taking place today. Nevertheless, the term *mercantilism* is still accepted for such purpose, and I prefer to use it to totally disentangle mercantilism from capitalism since they have nothing in common.

[6] Measured not just by the fraction of the GDP represented by government expenditure but by the number of state-run commanding heights of the economy.

and socialism of the 21st century.

Poverty

Trade barriers[7] block or hinder an easier access to a greater variety of products and services at better prices, hence they also increase the cost of living for the average citizen. Inefficient entrepreneurs and politicians have maintained these barriers in Venezuela for decades, with the excuse that "protecting" the national industry is of paramount importance which really hides their fear to compete. Nevertheless, the high cost imposed upon all Venezuelans, without their consent, is not part of the rhetoric of those who promote and defend this perverse protectionist logic.

Faría et al. (2005) estimated the static component of the annual cost imposed to consumers, derived from tariffs implemented in the textile, agricultural, steel and automobile sectors between 1990 and 1999. The results are shown in Table 1.

Sector	Total cost to consumers (USD)	Number of "protected" jobs by tariffs	Cost to consumers per "protected" job (USD)
Textiles	104,991,589	1,180	88,976
Agricultural	369,548,314	4,328	85,385
Steel	68,351,565	473	144,506
Automobiles	494,618,000	451	1,096,714

Table 1. Annual average cost to consumers per "protected" job.

Table 1 shows the cost each protected job represented to consumers -fourth column-. If tariffs were eradicated that cost could be understood as a gain for the consumers. Considering the worst scenario, where all the "protected" jobs of the different

---

[7] Such as high tariffs, customs obstacles, complex regulations, import prohibitions, quotas, safeguard laws, and others.

sectors were lost -if all tariffs were removed-, consumers would have gained the amounts indicated in the first column of Table 1, per year.

A simple arithmetic operation can prove that that gain would be of US$ 969,157,903 per year. By that time, the minimum wage oscillated around the US$ 2,400 annual level, reason why, Venezuelans could have paid those workers much better salaries and could still have earned profits[8].

In addition, free trade is a trigger of economic growth, which is the most effective and efficient mechanism to reduce poverty. It should have more importance in countries like Venezuela, where most of people are essentially poor. Nonetheless, the defense of consumers by official spokespersons of governments or enterprises is either conditioned or null in terms of reporting and dismantling the mercantilist operations that hinder free trade and make people poorer.

Venezuelan elites offer strong resistance to more protective institutions of the incomes and savings. Some of them are the dollarization of the economy or –better than that- an array of monetary freedom, which means to eliminate any legal tender law, enshrining the use of any currency as a constitutional right[9]. The reason behind this opposition is the inability to keep benefiting from the devaluation of the local currency. In a dollarized economy, the monetary control would not be in the hands of the national bureaucrats and technocrats, whose irresponsibili-ty has been prominent in the last sixty years. In the case of a monetary freedom system, with the bolívar (the local currency) still in circulation, devaluation could still happen but people would have multiple options to protect their savings and

---

[8] The same simple math logic proves that 6,432 workers would have lost their jobs but with US$ 969,157,903 of consumers' gains per year, meaning that each lost "protected worker" could have obtain up to US$ 150,677.54 per year.
[9] Including the possibility of issuing with backing from private banks

incomes from predation[10].

In the democratic era known as the "Fourth Republic", from 1958 to 1998, devaluation was a recurrent tool used by governments to finance the fiscal deficit[11]. It was also common to see mercantilist entrepreneurs declare in the press or on TV that the US dollar was overvalued and that devaluation was necessary to maintain the competitiveness of the local industry, with the most cynical indolence for the theft committed against citizens every time the bolivar was forced to lose value versus the US dollar. That theft reduces the international purchasing power of the average Venezuelan (because more bolívares would be needed to acquire the same single dollar to purchase abroad) and promotes a higher inflation level.

The current hyperinflationary disaster of the "Fifth Republic" period, from 1998 to the present time, is a consequence of the same devaluation policies, exacerbated, and of the fierce exchange control imposed by Chávez[12] since 2003, control from which – by the way – entrepreneurs close to power have benefitted in the acquisition of preferential dollars. Nowadays, Venezuela exhibits the highest inflation level of the planet[13].

Corruption

The judicial system is one of the most important counterweights of any democracy. The administration of impartial justice, independent of governments, is fundamental for the protection of the most basic rights, by effectively punishing their violations, that is, by generating healthy incentives to not break the rule of law. On the contrary, a judicial

---

[10] I prefer an array of monetary freedom without central bank, such as Panama's today.
[11] See Faría and Filardo, 2015
[12] N.E.: Maduro has kept the exchange control imposed by Chávez.
[13] N.E.: A deep explanation of Venezuela's inflation levels can be read in the Chapter 11 "Why should Venezuela embrace dollarization" by Steve Hanke in this book.

system subservient to the executive branch is prone to omitting limits and allowing bureaucrats to pervert judicial decisions[14].

The oil industry is another area in which corruption blooms. For those who make money under the shadow of the state – mercantilists – effectively transferring the property of PDVSA, the state-run oil company, to every citizen in the form of shares that could be traded in the international markets would also be a disadvantage, because it would be much more difficult to secure the privileges they have with the government as the absolute owner, if property were private and widespread[15].

Venezuelan elites also offer a strong resistance to let all the oil proceeds[16] be deposited directly upon the accounts of Venezuelans by birth and aged 21 years or older[17]. But, what they do not say is that, this measure would reduce the economic power of governments and would force them, to survive, to come to their citizens to negotiate the tax rate levied on those proceeds. Civil society, in turn, would have more power to demand services of higher quality, and one of the fundamental bases of a prosperous and long-lasting democracy would have been established: a government with an absolute fiscal dependence on its people[18].

It is worth making a brief digression at this point since I think

---

[14] See Faría and Montesinos, 2016.

[15] Econintech proposes a privatization program where an important number of shares would be sold to transnational companies interested in administering the oil business, with the purpose of gathering capital and generating efficiency.

[16] Paid to governments as taxes and royalties by the transnational companies for the exploration and exploitation activities they carry out.

[17] Besides monetary freedom and the property transfer of PDVSA to all Venezuelans, economist Hugo Faría has been promoting this initiative for almost two decades, and Econintech, as a think tank, since its foundation in 2015. This policy would last at least while a new simple and flat taxation system is implemented in Venezuela.

[18] At present, the government is 50% independent of its people because it directly receives oil proceeds.

it is the most controversial one. Detractors of the proposal of delivering all oil proceeds, in US dollars, directly to the people disseminate opinions based upon ridiculous ideas such as that "the people" are not trained, that an initiative like this would boost massive idleness or that such measure is populist.

Mercantilists and socialists underestimate the ability of Venezuelans because they fear to lose privileges granted by governments, and do not acknowledge the most inherent characteristic of the human nature: to respond to incentives[19]; so what is required to receive oil proceeds and limit the power of the state is to have formal institutions guaranteeing such objective, not intellectual training. These elites also omit the fact that all oil proceeds, in US dollars, divided by the number of Venezuelans by birth and aged 21 years or older would not be enough to just live off it, because the corresponding fraction for each citizen would be small. In other words, the argument of the massive boost of idleness seems to be more a sophism disseminated with the purpose of not implementing structural changes. Nevertheless, the fact that certain groups, exercising their right to freely choose, will opt for idleness is not discarded, but they would be forced to carry the consequences of such action, and the rules in force would allow them to learn.

This would be an empowerment policy far different from the previous populist measures of official spokesper-sons of the government and of the "opposition". Programs such as "Tarjeta mi Negra"[20] proposed by Manuel Rosales, or "Gotas de Petróleo"[21], that Maduro's regime has been trying to implement, consider delivering just part of the oil proceeds to the people, not all; and not in US dollars, but in bolívares. It is clear that generating an absolute fiscal dependence of the government on its citizens, limiting the state, and obstructting the emergence of corruption between inefficient entrepreneurs and bureaucrats, were not the goals of such populist proposals, but just continuing

---

[19] Mises, 1980.
[20] N.E.: "My Black Card" in English.
[21] N.E.: "Oil drops" in English.

23

to give people crumbs while the control of the economy is still kept in the hands of the political and economic elites, something very convenient for the already explained reasons.

Indoctrination

The sowing of ideological biases in the population, contrary to economic freedom, could be explained by considering the interests and incentives of the genesis of evil. Two effective mechanisms to achieve this doctrinal goal are available: the media and the educational system.

Because of its notorious disadvantage for the status quo, it is very unlikely that the media will provide access or cover ideas such as free international trade, the privatization of PDVSA, monetary freedom, tax simplification, relaxation of employment laws, and the reduction of the governmental size in general. On the contrary, it is very common to see socialist politicians and mercantilist entrepreneurs declare that such initiatives are unnecessary and unpatriotic. The intellectual floor provided by renowned economists is fundamental to generate an opinion matrix unfavorable to the ideas of freedom and prosperity that have worked all over the world.

The opposition to liberalism also exists in academia, where the schools of thought imposed as unquestionable truths are Keynesianism – and all of its derivatives[22] – and Marxism[23], both conducive to central planning and collectivization. Libertarian books and voices studied or listened at universities are really scarce.

---

[22] By the way, the self-called "liberals" or "center-right" politicians who are far away of the real classic liberalism or libertarianism count on well worldwide recognized economists followers of Marxism, Keynesianism, Neo-Keynesianism and Post-Keynesianism but you can never ever find an Austrian School, Chicago's School, or Public Choice School, Economist among their "counselors".

[23] See Faría and Filardo, 2015

Exclusion

The institutional framework of the last six decades has prevented the average Venezuelans from enjoying important benefits. The protection of their incomes and savings, the effective property of the oil business, the access to a wide variety of products and services available worldwide at lower prices, better paid jobs, higher exposure to new technologies, world class health and educational systems, an unconditional protection of private property, and better conditions to create new businesses, among others, are just some of the benefits from which the bulk of the population have been excluded in Venezuela. Definitely, the genesis of evil has prevented the common person from exercising one basic natural right: the freedom to choose. Disgraceful!

A fundamental reform fostering a rapid and sustainable economic growth, and a greater level of inclusion would be the best mechanism to eliminate the most serious problems of the population, and even to promote the cultural change that we require as a society. But such modification would be possible under the tutelage of a new leadership in the political, entrepreneurial and civic arenas. At Econintech, we are committed to contributing to the development of that libertarian leadership; full of confidence; not afraid to compete; supported by a strong belief in the power of markets, comparative advantages and efficiency, instead of in the power of political connections.

4. CAPITALISM AND ENTREPRENEURSHIP: AN ESSAY ON LATINAMERICA

By María Lorca-Susino

When we founded Econintech María Lorca-Susino was a great inspiration. A successful Spanish professional woman in the United States that believes and promotes freedom. Now, we are proud of having her as a member of the Board of Directors of Econintech. This is a short version of a working paper she wrote about the entrepreneurship in Latin America. She explains how the kleptocratic systems have affected the economies of this Region. The promotion of entrepreneurship in a country depend on many factors, but as Lorca-Susino states, the role of the president is critical because the high power that usually has in these countries, could incentive or discourage entrepreneurs. An important analysis that María does in her article is the differences, advantages, and disadvantages of presidential or parliamentarian government. María is Ph.D. and professor of Economics in the Business School at the University of Miami, CEO & Founder of MLS Academic Consulting.

The figure of the entrepreneur is a fundamental element in the equation of productivity and economic growth and its presence in the productive world depends on a series of business incentives such as the ease for the creation of a company, the action of government institutions to reward socially beneficial business activity, the criminalization of activity that goes against social welfare, and the existence of business incentives to encourage business action (Baumol et al., 2007) Therefore, the productive function depends directly on the figure of the entrepreneur and its relationship with business incentives that are linked to the type of economic organization system in each country. While the capitalist system has marginalized the option of communism as an efficient system of economic organization, capitalism has evolved throughout history from the capitalist islands of Venice and Genoa in the middle ages to the twentieth century where they developed different types of capitalism. Baumol et al (2007) explain that the capitalist system has many different forms that go from the "state-guided" typical of the countries of Southeast Asia, the oligarchic capitalism in Latin American countries, the "big-firm" capitalism developed in the United States, and finally the "entrepreneurial" capitalism in small geographic enclaves as in Silicon Valley in California. The only thing these capitalist systems have in common is that "they recognized the right of private ownership of property" while economic growth depends on the "mechanism of growth, innovation and entrepreneurship" (p.61) observed in each of these systems.

Capitalism and Entrepreneurship in Latin America: A Brief Study of the Current Situation

Most Latin American countries have an oligarchic capitalist system because, despite being a nominally capitalist system where the laws of private property are respected, the economic policies of governments do not prioritize economic growth to favor the population but to promote the economic interests of a privileged minority of the population.

These kleptocratic capitalist systems have several intrinsic characteristics in Latin American countries. These countries suffer from extreme inequality measurable by the Gini Coefficient, high informal activity studied by Soto (1989, 2000), a high level of corruption that hinder business development (Kaufman and Wei, 1999), and from the so-called "Dutch disease" due to the abundance of raw materials that helps strengthen vested interests making very difficult to break the stablished "client" system. (Friedman, 2005).

For oligarchic government, economic growth is not the priority, however, they tend to maintain a stable economic condition to avoid situations of social upheaval that could threaten the kleptocratic status quo. Therefore, these countries often suffer from large income differences measured by the Ginni Coefficient. The Word Bank[24] explains that the Gini Coefficient (Table 1) is still very high in the region but improving.

Country	Gini Coefficient in 2000	Gini Coefficient in year...	Difference
Argentina	51.1	41.4 (2014)	- 9.7
Chile	52.8	47.7 (2015)	-5.7
Colombia	58.7	50.8 (2016)	-7.9
México	51.4	43.4 (2016)	-8
Venezuela	48.2	46.2 (last year avialable 2006)	-2

Table 1: Gini Coeficient. Source: World Bank.

On the other hand, the oligarchic system is characterized by a high level of informal economic activity that affects the nation's economic growth. If informal activity were to be regulated, so that it could have access to credit and a business support network, the performance of these business could improve significantly with a positive effect on the nation's overall economic growth. However, informal economic activity can be understood as the end result of corruption, innate in this type of system and much more widespread than in the of "state-guided" system. Obstacles and difficulties found in the oligarchic system for the creation and development of any economic activity leads to corruption and, therefore, to informality as a way of avoiding corruption.

Corruption slows economic and entrepreneurial activity because with informality the entrepreneur is forced to have a lower productivity, a higher level of lost opportunity cost, a higher cost of doing business, which stops foreign investment

---

[24] World Bank: Gini Index.

from investing in a country since corruption is the equivalent of a 50% of taxes. (Wei, 2000) The "Corruption Perception Index, 2017" (Graph 3) published by Transparency International explains that all five countries analyzed have suffered a worsening of their corruption index between 2010[25] and 2017[26]. Graph 3 shows us that Chile is the country with best position with the lowest perception of corruption while Venezuela is the country with the highest perception index among the 180 countries analyzed in the study.

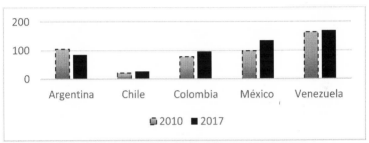

Figure 3: Corruption Perceptions Index. Source: Transparency International

Finally, in those countries with a high level of natural resources, the oligarchic capitalist system perpetuates itself since, as Thomas Friedman explained in "The First Law of Petropolitics," in oil-rich countries, "the Price of oil and the pace of freedom always move in opposite directions. "(Friedman, 2005, 31)

These three actors of the oligarchic capitalist system are related to the figure of the president. The choice of the type of constitutional systems in Latin America, a parliamentary or presidential system, is a fundamental decision since each one has its advantages and disadvantages. Professor Juan Linz (1996) explains that the parliamentary system fosters democratic consolidation in those nations with deep political divisions and numerous political parties. At the same time, Linz explains that

---

[25] See Transparency International CPI 2010
[26] See Transparency International CPI 2017

the biggest problem of the presidential system is that both, the president and the legislators of the Congress, are elected by the people; thus, they both claim to have the legitimacy to govern. This situation creates destabilizing competition and tensions between the two branches of government, particularly in nascent democracies. In a presidential system, the presidential candidate is directly responsible to his constituents and during the electoral campaign he informs about his political vision while, in a parliamentary system, the candidate and policies are left to the decision of the political party after the elections. One of the dangers of the presidential system is "hyper-presidentialism" where the president is directly elected by the voters, so that he has his own fixed electoral mandate separate from the electoral mandate of the legislature. Thus, the president has the right to choose the ministers of their choice regardless of the composition of the congress and can take his mandate to such an extreme that poses questions of its democratic legitimacy. (Stepan and Skach, 1993, Mainwaring and Soberg Shugart, 1997.

In Latin America, political power has traditionally been concentrated in the figure of the president who holds all the power and who is subject to few effective restrictions, which weakens both democracy and good governance. This explains that the Democracy Index (2018) classifies Chile, Argentina, Colombia, and Mexico as "flawed democracy" while Venezuela as "authoritarian democracy." Table 2 shows that the measurement of the "electoral process and political pluralism" for all these five countries are quite favorable, except for Venezuela. Favorable results for the "electoral process and political pluralism" metric are not understood when analyzed with the low results for "political participation". For example, in Colombia "political participation" is only 5 points while the score of the "electoral process and pluralism" ranks at 9.17. Similarly, Chile shows a very low "political participation" result of 4.49 points while in "process and electoral pluralism" qualifies with an impressive 9.58 points. Finally, the metric for "government functioning" shows that except in Chile, the governments of Mexico, Colombia and Venezuela have a lot of work to do, especially in Argentina. Special mention requires Venezuela for its low score in all of the metrics presented in table 2. Although the result for "political participation" in Venezuela resonates with Chile and Colombia, the other two metrics are extremely low as the result of the political situation suffered in the country for the past two decades.

The economy of many European absolute monarchies, during the 16th, 17th and first half of the 18th centuries, centered on a system of monopoly concessions, monetary control, export subsidy, import prohibitions, heavy tax burden, and control of natural resources. The ultimate objective of such system, referred to as mercantilism, was the accumulation of wealth – in the form of gold – by the crown. Nowadays, with the exception that gold is not money anymore and that monarchies were replaced by other forms of government (in some despicable cases, with almost absolute power as well), most of the mentioned vices survive[27].

Country	Electoral process and pluralism	Functioning of government	Political participation
Noruega	10	9.62	10
Chile	9.58	8.57	4.49
Argentina	9.17	5.36	6.11
Colombia	9.17	6.79	5
México	8.33	6.07	7.22
Venezuela	1.67	1.79	4.45

Table 2: Democracy index by category. Source: Democracy Index 2018

In Latin America, hyper-presidentialism is the type of governmental organization with a president also being the

---

[27] Above all in the United States of America, *crony capitalism* is the combination of terms used to describe the mercantilist practices taking place today. Nevertheless, the term *mercantilism* is still accepted for such purpose, and I prefer to use it to totally disentangle mercantilism from capitalism since they have nothing in common.

commander in chief of the armed forces at the same time as the head of state, so the president is much more than an executive head. (Morgenstern, Polga-Hecimovich, and Shair-Rosenfield, 2013) This poses the biggest problem for democratic consolidation. (Gargarella, 2013). Therefore, in most Latin American countries, presidents tend to accumulate powers, both legislative and non-legislative which O'Toole synthesized in table 3. (Gavin O'Toole 137, 2017).

| **Very High:** Chile, Ecuador, Brazil |
| **Medium High:** Argentina, México, República Dominicana, El Salvador, Panamá |
| **Medium Low:** Bolivia, Costa Rica, Honduras, Nicaragua, Paraguay, Perú, Uruguay |
| **Very Low:** Colombia, Venezuela, Guatemala |

Table 3: Overall Presidential Powers. Source: Gavin O'Toole, Politics Latin America.

In addition, the history of most of the countries of the area is also highly linked to the economic role played by the theory of import substitution industrialization (ISI) developed by Raúl Prebisch in the 50's with the idea of protecting the so-called "infant industries"— that were mostly in the hands of the oligarch minority—from international competition during the process of industrial growth. Table 4 analyzes the evolution of economic growth during the years in which ISI was the economic policy for development and economic growth and during years of free trade. The result shows that in Argentina, Colombia, Mexico and Venezuela economic growth has been lower during the free market years where government protection did not exist. In Chile, however, experienced more economic growth during the free market years than during the period of the ISI.

The reason why economic growth is lower during the free trade years can be explained by many factors. One of them is the evolution and role played by entrepreneurs and entrepreneurship activity. The Global Entrepreneurship and Development Institute

(GEDI)[28] publishes the Global Entrepreneurship Index (GEI) which analyzes the business position of 138 countries worldwide. Figure 4 shows that Chile is the best positioned country in Latin America followed by Colombia, which, in turn, are the two countries with the best economic growth during the years of free trade (Table 4). However, Venezuela is the worst positioned in the GEI and the country with the worst growth during the free trade years.

Country	Average Economic Growth during ISI (1960-80)	Average Economic Growth during "free trade" 1980-2000
Argentina	1.94	0.42
Chile	1.87	3.2
Colombia	2.72	1.13
México	3.35	0.75
Venezuela	0.18	-1.01

Table 4: Average Economic Growth per Capita. Source: Bloomberg

A more detailed analysis of the data shown (figure 4) that the entrepreneurship spirit in these five countries worsened between 2014 and 2017. While Chile's global position deteriorated from 15th out of 138 in 2014 to position 19 in 2017, Venezuela suffered the most dramatic declined raking 92 out of 138 countries in 2014 to 126 in 2017. Colombia's entrepreneurship level went from place 24 in 2014 to place 43 in 2016 to place 47 in 2017. The global position for Mexico in the competitiveness index is very interesting because it shows a great deal of fluctuation. The country was in place 57th in 2014 but significantly lost competitiveness ranking 87th in 2016 to improve in 2017 reaching the 75th position. Argentina has gone from the 56th position in 2014, to the 61st position in 2016, to the 88th place in 2017.

---

[28] Website of the Global Entrepreneurship and Development Institute.

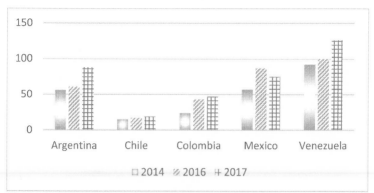

Figure 4: GEI World Rank for Chile, Colombia, México, Argentina and Venezuela. Source: Global Entrepreneurship Index.

The GEI measures different factors to calculate the level of entrepreneurship. Figure 5 presents how Chile, Colombia, Mexico, Argentina and Venezuela perform in four specific factors. First of all, the "opportunity startup" measures the possibilities that companies find in order to launch their business project, regardless of whether they are innovative or repetitive production companies. In this metric, Chile is the country that stands out the most, followed by Mexico and Colombia, while the level of Venezuela is insignificant. The "competition" factor measures the level of competition existing in the country so that companies can carry out their business work. It is important to point out that all the countries analyzed have very similar levels, which undoubtedly explains a lot the entrepreneurship results. Process and product Innovation are two important metrics. While "process innovation" is quite low for all five countries, "product innovation" is curiously higher; a difference that can be explained by analyzing the "human capital factor" (human capital); the higher the human capital the higher product innovation but not necessarily process innovation. Chile, Colombia and Argentina are the best positioned countries.

Figure 5: GEI for 2017 by Individual Factors. Source: Global Entrepreneurship Index

All these entrepreneurial factors together explain that Chile and Colombia are the two countries with the highest new business density which measures how many new businesses are registered per 1,000 people[29] (Graph 6). It is important to note that there is no business creation data for Venezuela in this series, so Venezuela has not been included in this chart.

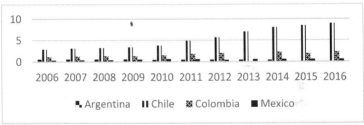

Figure 6: New Business Density (New Registrations per 1,000 people ages 15-64). Source: World Bank

Final Words

This work emphasizes that there is a relationship between economic growth and entrepreneurial activity which defends the figure of the entrepreneur as a fundamental element in the equation of productivity and economic growth. At the same time, this paper presents that there is a relationship between the

---

[29] https://data.worldbank.org/indicator/IC.BUS.NDNS.ZS

entrepreneur and his productive function and the incentives, or lack thereof, to undertake entrepreneurial work. The entrepreneurial activity is affected by the action of government institutions to reward socially beneficial business activity, the criminalization of activity that goes against social welfare, and by the existence of business incentives.

This study concludes that during the free trade years, Chile was the country with the highest economic growth followed by Colombia, Mexico, Argentina and Venezuela. Also, this study indicates that Chile was the country with the highest rank in the government functioning index, which better functioning there is more transparency, which helps fight against the political corruption which determine entrepreneurial activity and business creation. In this way, Chile is the country with the best functioning of the government while enjoying the lowest level of corruption helping the country obtain a competitive position in the "Doing Business Index."

Mexico is a very interesting country to analyze in these three dimensions. Mexico has the second best record when measuring the country's political functioning, but it suffers from the second worst index of corruption and despite this, it has the best result in the "Doing Business Index". These results show a number important interesting political and economic contradictions.

Venezuela, however, is the country with a "government functioning" index that really explains the situation of political dictatorship endured by the country and, therefore, suffers from the highest level of corruption and is the last countries in the "Doing Business" raking.

With these political and economic data in perspective, Chile is the country with the highest business creation reflected in the Global Entrepreneurial Index (GEI), followed by Colombia, Mexico, Argentina and Venezuela.

	Chile	Colombia	México	Argentina	Venezuela
Economic Growth	3.2	1.13	0.75	0.42	-1.01
Doing Business	56	65	54	119	189
Corruption Index	26	96	135	85	169
Electoral process and pluralism	9.58	9.17	9.17	8.33	1.67
Functioning of government	8.57	5.36	6.07	6.79	1.75
Elctoral Participation	4.49	6.11	7.22	5	4.45
GEI	1	2	3	4	5
Business Density	1	2	3	4	5

Table 5: Final Findings. Source: Author's Elaboration

5. VENEZUELA: FROM RICHES TO RAGS.
THE REAL HISTORY

By Rafael Acevedo & Luis Cirocco

This article is the partial transcription of our speech, Venezuela: From Riches to Rags, lectured at the Mises University program in the summer of 2017, which was a milestone for Econintech; my part, for instance, was reproduced 2.5 million times on the Mises Institute Facebook page. We shall always thank that institute for the opportunity they provided us with to participate in such a prestigious program of Austrian Economics. Right after that, I have had the chance to lecture this conference at other important places too, such as University of Miami; Texas Tech University; Florida Southern College; in a PodCast for Warwick University in UK; in interviews for Students for Liberty Colombia; on the online magazine Wellington in Mexico; in written interviews in Australia, New Zealand, and go on. I think people like this conference because we talk clearly and honestly, which is possible just because Econintech has no ties with cronies or current politicians. The only dream we pursue is the implementation of a real free-market economy in our country.

In order to understand the disaster unfolding in Venezuela, we need to journey through the most recent century of our history and look at how our institutions deteriorated over time. It is simple and easy to notice that Venezuela once enjoyed high levels of economic freedom, although this mostly occurred under dictatorial regimes. Nevertheless, when Venezuela embraced democracy, politicians began to kill economic freedom, not all at once, of course, but through a gradual process. We embarked on democracy at the expense of the economic welfare of millions of people.

And, ultimately, the paramount lesson we learned is that socialism never ever works, no matter what Paul Krugman, Joseph Stiglitz, guys in Spain like Pablo Iglesias, or in the US like Bernie Sanders –or recently like Mrs. Ocasio-Cortez– say. It was very common –during the years of Hugo Chávez's mandate– to hear pundits, politicians, and economists declare on TV that this time "socialism is being put into practice properly". This time, many Venezuelans figured it out.

They were and are still wrong!

There was a time when this country was quite prosperous and wealthy, when Venezuela was even referred to as an "economic miracle" in many academic books and scientific papers. In this regard, by the way, we strongly recommend to read the book –available online in Spanish on our website www.econintech.org– "Causes and Culprits of Venezuela's Disaster: A Homage to Hugo Faría", edited by Rafael Acevedo and Luis Cirocco with the collaboration of great academicians of the free-market movement, to better understand the roots of the current situation developing in our country.

During those years of flourishing prosperity, of the five presidents we had, four were dictators and generals of the army. Our civil and political rights were restricted then: we had neither freedom of the press nor universal suffrage, for instance. Nevertheless, while we lived mostly under dictatorships, we still could enjoy high levels of economic freedom. So, Venezuelans were not in a misery condition as they are today, and we state that the so-mentioned argument that Venezuela changed to a better country for its entire people is not consistent with reality at all.

In general, Venezuela changed to a better condition just for those people directly involved in politics or with political connections. In a phrase, socialists in power changed the scenario for their own benefit. Nonetheless, in the economic field, the story was quite different. Although Venezuelan "Ivy Leaguers" (mostly Keynesian economists) try to underestimate us brandishing their half-million-dollar degrees, we will keep demonstrating and saying that the current economic, social and political disaster started in 1958, with the implementation of the democratic socialist agenda –now known as Cultural Marxism– which involved policies still promoted nowadays. Hence, local socialists and their advisors were and are still wrong in terms of the scope of the change they have boosted.

A Brief Economic History of Venezuela

Many people believe in what is disseminated through the media or by the elites interested in not implementing structural economic changes. So, countering such instilled bias is our real pleasure when we talk about our country everywhere. Those biased views just focus on the last 20 years and never explain that Venezuela had the same problems before Chávez, with lower intensity maybe, but rooted in the same perverse structure of incentives. Rafael normally compares the situation of our country with a terminal cancer patient, who, at this moment, is dying. Politicians, cronies, traditional advisors, influencers, and the "liberals of the *status quo*" blame just the strong tobacco that the patient started smoking in 1999 as the only culprit of the lung cancer, but do not say that the same patient started smoking 10 packs a day of slightly soft cigarettes since 1958. For this reason, it is of paramount importance to explore the recent history of Venezuela.

The economic miracle indeed began a century ago when, from 1914 to 1922, Venezuela entered the international oil race. In 1914, the first oil well went into production. Fortunately, the government did not make the mistake of attempting to manage the business. The wells were privately owned and, in many cases, owned by international companies which operated within the country.

There were tax incentives and other so-called concessions
40

employed to promote the exploration and exploitation of oil. Most industries –including the oil one– remained private. It is worth mentioning that Venezuela was not in a total *laissez-faire* frame, of course. Moreover, during this period, tax rates in the country were relatively low.

In 1957, the marginal tax rate on individuals was 12 percent. There was certainly a state presence, but the public sector just absorbed around 20 percent of the GDP. Nevertheless, government spending was mainly used to build the country's basic infrastructure.

The area of international trade was quite free as well –and *very* free compared to today's. There were relatively high tariffs, but no other major barriers to trade such as quotas, anti-dumping laws, or safeguards. Of course, economic elites existed but their influence and "power" in the political arena was very low because, at the end of the day, a dictator[58] does not need economic favors from cronies. From our standpoint, cronies –or as we call them in colloquial Spanish "Empresaurios[59]"– were another group benefitted by the political change of 1958, because their influence started expanding and their wealth increasing, not because they efficiently served people with better quality products at better prices, but thanks to protectionist institutions.

Nevertheless, during the period concerned, there were just a few state-owned companies and virtually no price controls, no rent controls, no interest-rate controls, and no exchange-rate controls.

---

[58] In our view, a dictator, like General Marcos Pérez Jiménez, is conceptually far different from a tyrant, like Chávez or Maduro.

[59] N.E.: This word does not exist in Spanish; it is just a "game of words" resulting from the combination of the terms "businessmen" and "dinosaurs". Another term commonly used in the same sense is "Empresucios", which is another "game of words" resulting from the combination of "dirty" and "businessmen" both terms are used in reference of cronies.

We were not free from the problems typically caused by a central bank either. In 1939, Venezuela created its own central bank, but it functioned –to a great extent– just to defend an irrevocable fixed exchange rate with the US dollar.

Moving Toward More Interventionism

Despite the high levels of economic freedom that existed during those years, governmental legislation started to chip away at that freedom. The implemented changes included the nationalization of the telephone company, the creation of numerous state-owned companies and state-owned banks with the purpose of "developing the country". The Venezuelan government thus began sowing the seeds of destruction, and the progressive deterioration of the economy became more evident. We understand that some "strategic sectors" were taken by Gen. Marcos Pérez Jiménez (MPJ), such as Telecom, because as in any dictatorship communications are censored.

In 1958, Venezuela embraced democracy when MPJ was overthrown. With this political change, all the normal benefits of democracy showed up, such as freedom of the press, universal suffrage, and other civil rights. Unfortunately, these reforms came along with the continued destruction of our economic freedom, and that did not have to happen.

The first democratically elected president was Rómulo Betancourt. He was a communist turned into a social democrat. In fact, while he was in exile, he was instrumental in the foundation of the Communist Party in Costa Rica and helped found the Communist Party in Colombia as well. Not surprisingly, as president, he started destroying the economic institutions we had, by implementing price controls, rent controls, and other regulations. On top of that, he and his allies created a new constitution that was hostile to private property.

In spite of this –or perhaps because of this– Betancourt is almost universally revered in Venezuela as "the father of our democracy." This remains true even today as Venezuela collapses.

Indeed, we had far greater economic freedom under Betancourt than we have in today's Venezuela. But, all of the presidents who came after Betancourt took similar positions and continued to chip away at our institutions. The only exception was Carlos Andrés Pérez who, in his second term, attempted some kind of liberalization reforms. But he performed these later reforms so badly and haphazardly that markets turned out being blamed for the resulting crises. As Rothbard said "freeing only a few areas at a time will only impose continuous distortions that will cripple the workings of the market and discredit it in the eyes of an already fearful and suspicious public" (p.66). In addition, Carlos Andrés' counselors seemed to be more worried about affecting their crony friends than affecting the citizens. They, then, increased the disbelief and mistrust on capitalism, reason why, perhaps, they have been some of the great culprits that Venezuelans misunderstand what real freedom is.

The Rise of Chavismo: the Predicament of Destructionism...

Over time, the gradual destruction of economic freedom led to more and more impoverishment and crisis. This, in turn, set the stage for the rise of a political outsider with a populist message: Hugo Chávez. He was elected in 1998 and promised to replace our "lighter" socialism by a form of hard socialism, which he called "the revolution of the 21st century" and which only magnified the problems we had faced for decades. He was able to pass an even more anti-private property constitution. Since Chávez's death in 2013, the attacks against private property continued, and Chávez's successor, Nicolás Maduro, keeps promising more of the same. The government has turned toward outright authoritarian socialism, and Maduro's intent is to pass a new constitution, according to which private property is practically abolished and he can remain in power for life.

A Legacy of Poverty

So, what are the results of socialism in Venezuela? We have

experienced hyperinflation; people eating garbage; schools that do not teach; hospitals that do not heal; long and humiliating lines to buy flour, bread, or basic medicines; and the militarization of practically every aspect of life. The cost of living has skyrocketed in recent years. The latest Dr. Steve Hanke's estimation of the annual inflation was 149,013% (circa March 2019). Yes, there is nothing wrong with your eyes..., more than one hundred and forty-nine thousand percent in a year.

Now, we are enabled to show some numbers relative to the daily life of a professional in Venezuela. We will present the cost of some goods and services in terms of a salary earned by a full public university professor[60]. In the 1980s, our full professor needed almost 15 minutes of his salary to buy one kilogram of beef. Today, in July 2017, he needs to pay the equivalent of 18 hours to buy the same amount of beef. During the 1980s, our full professor needed almost one year of his salary for a new sedan. In July 2017, he must pay the equivalent of 25 years of his salary (and in March 2019 he needs more than 93 years to buy a 10,000 US$ sedan). In the 1980s, the same professor could buy 17 basic baskets of essential goods with his monthly salary. In July 2017, he could buy just one-quarter of a basic basket (and in March 2019, just one-fifth of it).

And what about the value of our money? In March 2007, the largest denomination of paper money in Venezuela was the 100 bolívares bill. With it, 28 US dollars, 288 eggs, or 56 kilograms of rice could be bought. Today, 0.01 dollars, 0.2 eggs, and 0.08 kilograms of rice could be bought. In July 2017, five 100 bolívares bills were required to buy just one egg. And just for informational purposes, in March 2019, the purchasing "egg" power of that 100 bolívares bill is $5.45*10^{-9}$. Yes again! There is nothing wrong with your eyes. That is a number expressed in

---

[60] When we updated this article, a quick research showed that the minimum salary of a full professor in the USA oscillates around 120,000.00 US$ per year, while in Venezuela is around 30,000.00 Bs monthly, which represents something like 8.60 US$ at the black market exchange rate.

scientific notation, which means 0 point EIGHT ZEROS, and then 545 egg.

As can be easily deducted, socialism is the cause of Venezuelan misery. Citizens are starving, eating garbage, losing weight. Children are malnourished. Most of the people in Venezuela would be happy to eat out of America's trashcans; it would be considered gourmet.

And, what is the response of our society? Well, it is the young people who are leading the fight for freedom in Venezuela, no matter what the current political leaders tell them to do. They do not want to be called "the opposition." They are the resistance, in Spanish, "La Resistencia." They are the real heroes of freedom in our country, but the world needs to know that they are being killed by a tyrannical government, and all members of the resistance are persecuted on a daily basis.

Nevertheless, new pro-market leadership must emerge before we can expect any major change to occur. Our current political opposition parties also hate free markets, including the current Interim President's party, Voluntad Popular, the same of Leopoldo López, which belongs to the International Socialist since its foundation. Its leaders have publicly declared that they are proud socialists or those self-called "central-right" leaders. They do not like Maduro, but they still want their version of socialism to be implemented. They adore the 1999 constitution and want to coordinate a government which includes Chávez's supporters.

This is not surprising. The poor understanding of Venezuelans about the importance of freedom and free markets has created our current disaster. We, Venezuelans, never understood freedom in its broader dimension because when we enjoyed high levels of economic freedom, we allowed the destruction of political and civil rights, and when we finally established democracy, we allowed the destruction of economic freedom.

Despite all this, there is still reason for hope. Many young students are committed to working for our cause. Econintech has done an excellent promotion of real pro-free-market reforms, required to eradicate not only the current crisis but also the root of evil, socialism. Our network has increased since our foundation in 2015; now, we have excellent partners, friendly institutions, allies, collaborators, and –maybe someday– many donors believing in our work. We are not concerned about not influencing the current traditional politicians since they are so tied to socialism that it could result in a waste of time. We bet for the next generation, young people as leaders and professionals of Movimiento Libertad Venezuela, Rumbo Libertad, and many other groups which seem to be authentic and the future of the free-market institutions in Venezuela. We strongly believe that our country can become the Georgia of Latin America, which after a crony Social-Democracy in its first post-communist years, was able to understand that a radical pro-free-

PART 2: SUCCESFUL CURES

6. POLAND: STABILIZATION AND REFORMS UNDER EXTRAORDINARY POLITICS
By Leszek Balcerowicz

In a book about what Venezuela needs to achieve Prosperity and Liberty –after the tyranny-, it is important to have a succesful example of radical reforms applied in a post-communist country. And Poland is one of the better. Dr. Balcerowics talks about his experience as Minister of Finance and analyses the results of the radical reforms of his economic program. This is an extract of the article "Poland: stabilization and reforms under extraordinary and normal politics" by Balcerowics. Professor Leszek is former Deputy Prime Minister of Poland (1989 -1991, 1997-2000) and President of the Central Bank of Poland (2001-2007). He is Professor of Economics at Warsaw School of Economics, and founder of FOR (Civil Development Forum) a think tank that promotes freedom. He, directly, authorized me to include this short version of his article.

I accepted in 1978 request of Józef Sołdaczuk, the head of the Institute for International Economics at the Central School of Planning and Statistics (the CSPS[61]) where I worked, to help him to establish an economic policy unit at the central party institute. The name of the institute was awful (the Institute of Marxism and Leninism) and I was very unhappy about that[62]. However, the work we did had nothing to do with Marxist ideology: we were warning that Poland was facing a grave economic crisis resulting from an inherent inefficiency of socialist economy and to the accumulated foreign debt, and we called for radical changes in the economic policy.

---

61 Since 1990 Warsaw School of Economics (WSE).
62 I left the institute in May 1980 just before the outbreak of Solidarity movement.

Parallel to that I created at the WSE an informal group of younger economists. We met regularly once a week, and I tried to make sure that we had very thorough discussions of all the important segments of the institutional system: the enterprise sector, the financial system, the foreign trade regime, local governments, etc. The proposed model, which emerged from our discussions and which I described in a synthetic text, could be described as a market economy based on labor – managed firms.

The proposed reforms were publicly presented in September 1980, just after the appearance of the Solidarity movement. The new situation created a huge demand for the 'social' (i.e. unofficial) proposals for reforms, and we were the only ones who systematically worked on that for more than two years. As a result, the media started to speak about the 'Balcerowicz team', and Solidarity largely accepted our economic proposal. The festival of Solidarity ended with the introduction of the Martial Law on Dec. 13, 1981.

The meetings of the group continued in the 1980, but this time we did not care about any political realism, and discussed such fundamental topics as liberalization, privatization, capital markets, foreign trade regime. We dedicated less time to the tax system and to the welfare state. All this was a very interesting hobby – we did not see any light at the end of the tunnel. However, by chance we were doing an important part of our 'homework' which became practically relevant in the second half of 1989. A general lesson is that one should be prepared for the window of opportunity by pursuing what appears to be a useless hobby.

In the spring of 1989 I wrote a paper on the policies for Poland's economy. They included rapid and massive liberalization, convertibility of Polish zloty, tough and quick macro-stabilization, the fastest possible stabilization, etc[63].

---

[63] Stefan Kawalec, the member of the original Balcerowicz team, and my closest economic advisor, wrote a similar paper in 1988 while I was in Germany (Kawalec, 1989).

While writing this I had no idea that a few months later I would be in charge of Poland's stabilization and transformation program.

Radical stabilization and reforms under the period of extraordinary politics

In the late August 1989 I was asked by the Prime Minister-designate to become his 'Ludwig Erhard'[64]. I first refused and then accepted. There were several reasons for my final decision. First, I felt that, by chance, I made an important part of the homework necessary for the job. Second, there was a team with whom I worked in the past years on whose members I could rely in a government job. Without the presence of the team I would not have accepted Mazowiecki's offer. Third, I made clear that I was only interested in a tough stabilization and radical transformation of the economy, and this position was accepted by the Prime Minister.

Fourth, I asked to be the chairman of the Economic Committee of the Council of Ministers so as to be able to coordinate the economic policy of all ministers, and he agreed, too. Finally, he also accepted that I would have an important say in choosing the economic ministers, and indeed most of them were my own choice; there was nobody to whom I would have objected.

I had no problem with articulating the goals of the economic program. The short term goal was to eliminate the catastrophic imbalances and the resulting hyperinflation. The longer term goal was to catch up with the West. The first goal was to be mostly achieved by rapid and radical tightening of fiscal and monetary policies, and the second by a comprehensive transformation, which I divided into massive liberalization, including currency convertibility, and deeper institutional charge

---

[64] I knew from my previous studies of Erhard reforms that the job in Poland was much more difficult and comprehensive.

(SOE's[65] privatization, setting up the stock exchange, restructuring of the public administration, etc.). Liberalization was also necessary to remove massive shortages.

*

In working out and in analyzing the policies I used a simple analytical scheme which consisted of four variables:

The <u>initial conditions</u> in Poland turned out to be even more dramatic than I expected. On my third day in the job I learned that the previous government has spent the substantial hard currency savings of the people deposited in the state banks (obviously, I had to be silent on that; the surprising surge in our exports during 1990 helped to pay back this debt). Also, I did not realize how large was another part of the domestic debt – that in the form of the payments people made for cars and apartments without obtaining them under socialism.

The <u>external conditions</u> turned out to be difficult to predict, and in 1991 took the form of huge shocks (the war in the Persian Gulf and the related increases in the price of oil).

In contrast, I did not find it difficult to determine the <u>desired end-state</u>. With respect to the macro-economy it was just low inflation and a reasonably balanced budget. Except for the early 1970s, when I was under influence of Keynesianism, I never believed in the virtue of fiscal stimulation of the economy and I was strongly focused on the longer term growth and, thus, on the supply side reforms. The whole transformation after socialism was about the supply side. (This is why the conventional Western macro-economics, with its focus on the demand side, was ill prepared to deal with the reforms after socialism).

I did not find it difficult in 1989 to determine what should be the targeted institutional system of the economy which served as a guide-post for the reforms. It was clear to me that we should target the system capable of ensuring rapid and sustained

---

[65] N.E: State-Owned Entreprises.

catching up with the West. And based on my previous studies I was pretty sure about the general features of such system: predominantly private, with intense competition, outward oriented, based on general rules, macro-economically stable. One could easily derive from this description the main directions of the necessary reforms, especially massive privatization and liberalization of the economy.

However, starting in 1991, I came to the conclusion that there were important gaps in my knowledge about the target system. (This was also true, I think, of the other members of the economic team). I did not know enough about the welfare state and especially the pension system. This probably helps to explain why no deeper social spending reforms were included in the package of reforms enacted in Dec. 1989, and – what was worse – why the fiscally destructive proposals of the Ministry of Labor were not stopped by the economic team. The second gap referred to the tax system. This in turn explains why we accepted in 1990 the IMF's proposal of conventional progressive personal income tax with three rates by the team.

The true intellectual and practical challenges were present with respect to some aspects of the optimal transition policies, i.e. policies capable of bringing the economy from the desperate initial conditions to the desired target system. I have to distinguish here the general strategy (i.e. what should be the content and the timing of the whole package of the policies) and the specification of some transition policies.

On the first issue, I have always regarded the popular juxtaposition of 'shock therapy versus gradualism' as pseudoscientific nonsense which has obstructed clear thinking and served as an instrument of anti-reform propaganda. The very expression 'shock' therapy frightens ordinary people and, indeed, has been often used for that purpose. 'Gradualism', in turn, is hopelessly vague. The juxtaposition 'shock therapy versus gradualism' is incapable of expressing the most important problems when faced with the choice of the economic strategy after the collapse of socialism. This is why, from the very beginning, I have been using a different conceptual apparatus[66].

First, I distinguished between the two types of policies: macro-stabilization (S) and institutional transformation (T) which, in turn, I divided into liberalization (L), i.e. enlarging the scope of economic freedom and a deeper institutional change (I), e.g. privatization of the state-owned enterprises, setting up an independent central bank or transforming the public administration. Second, I noticed that these policies differ in their maximum possible speed: S and L can bring much faster results than most of I.

There were some more specific issues which gave rise to debates and/or uncertainties:

I regarded the privatization of the economy (i.e. an increasing share of the private sector) as an absolutely necessary fundamental reform, both of economic and practical nature. And I considered fast 'transformational' privatization, i.e. privatizing the inherited SOE's as its essential component[67].

Even though I was for the fast privatization it was obvious to me that the radical approach to reforms we chose (i.e. starting S, L and T policies about the same time), implied that the stabilization had to be introduced in a predominantly socialist economy, as privatization unavoidably takes more time that S and L policies.

I was also convinced that given the early hyperinflation we had to quickly introduce a tough stabilization program. And being aware the constellation of forces typical of the SOE's: no private owners interested in profits and thus resisting the wage

---

[66] For more on the criticism of the 'shock therapy' and gradualism and on the alternative conceptual framework see: Balcerowicz, 1992, p. 4-6 and 1995.

[67] However, the post-communist governments which ruled in Poland late 1993-1997 seemed to consider the corporatization and mergers of SOE's of a substitute of privatization

pressures we introduced tough tax-based wage controls. However, I was still uncertain about the reaction of the state-dominated economy to the radical economic program and especially about its supply response.

I considered the unification of the rate exchange and the introduction of its convertibility (within the current account operations as a crucial element of the policy package). I also accepted that the rate of exchange introduced at the beginning of 1990 should serve as a nominal anchor in the stabilization policy and thus should be maintained for a certain time.

Around the middle of 1990 it turned out that the implemented program was more restrictive than planned, and we had a debate within the economic team, on what should be policy response. Most of my advisers, including Stanisław Gomułka, whom I trusted very much (and continue to do) suggested that some relaxation of fiscal and monetary policy may be in order, and this was done. However, when, after a rapid decline in the first half of 1990, inflation started to increase in the autumn of this year, the monetary policy was tightened again – in spite of the coming presidential elections.

In line with my expectations the radical program brought about a quick removal of massive shortages and a rapid decline of inflation. However the correctional rise in prices in January 1990 was much higher that forecasted, and the statistical decline in GDP during 1990 much deeper. This data fuelled some early criticism of the program. A bit later I realized that the official data exaggerated the decline in GDP as they largely omitted the fast-growing private sector.

*

In the second half of 1991, another electoral campaign, this time preceding the Parliamentary elections, was raging. More than 60 parties participated in this campaign, and most of them were critical of the economic program, condemning what they called excessive 'monetarism' and the 'Balcerowicz plan', and exploiting economic problems. In the new Parliament 6-8 parties were required to form a government. I left the government office on 18 Dec., 1991, very tired and without intention ever to return to it. I was still convinced that to choose a non-radical strategy would have been a terrible error but I was uncertain about the supply side response of the economy. A bit later, more and more information started to appear that GDP was on its way back to growth.

*

I think that the choice of radical strategy was correct and I base this statement on my reading of the empirical literature on the post-socialist economies: I am not able to find a single example of clearly non-radical strategy (delayed reforms and/or stabilization, slower pace of S and L policies, etc.) which - for the similar initial and external conditions - would have produced superior outcomes. In particular, I have always regarded the thesis 'institutions were neglected' as a pretentious claim directed against radical strategy[68], similar to the juxtaposition: 'shock therapy versus gradualism'.

However, the implemented policies negatively deviated in some important aspects from my original intentions (and those of other members of the economic team). Some of these deviations can be termed errors, i.e. they were avoidable if certain conditions, which were not completely unrealistic, were present. All the major error were committed by omission, i.e. the economic team, including the Ministry of Finance, accepted wrong proposals from some other ministries, especially the Ministry of Labor, who was in charge of social policies. Therefore, contrary to many other post-socialist countries, the pensioners in Poland were overprotected. However, the popular view in Poland, strengthened by populist politicians, was that it

---

[68] First, those who made such a claim usually define 'institutions' in a very narrow way, excluding radical extension of economic freedom via liberalization from the domain of institutional charge .Second, they are empirically wrong even on their narrow concept of institutions, as countries which have introduced more of S and L also introduced more of deeper institutional change. (For more on this see Hartwell, 2013)

were pensioners who were especially hard hit by the 'shock therapy'.

Another error, fiscally less destructive, was to accept the proposal of a special pension system for the farmers (this system is still awaiting reform.) Finally, we did not stop the overgenerous system of unemployment benefits, proposed by the Ministry of Labor, which granted these benefits to the graduates of the schools and universities, thus inflating the number of the unemployed.

I realized a couple of years later that we could probably have introduced in the early 1990 a simple flat tax instead of accepting the IMF proposal for the conventional progressive personal income tax and introducing it in 1992. I consider it as an error. It resulted from the lack of knowledge on my part and among other members of the economic team (I don't remember anybody proposing a flat tax in Poland in 1989-91).

The pace of SOE's privatization was much slower than I wanted. This deviation was very difficult to avoid due to political calendar in Poland. Janusz Lewandowski[69], who started in early 1991, tried to work out the scheme of mass privatization. However, before it was implemented, the parliamentary elections, in the autumn of 1991 came and Lewandowski resigned his post. Later, due to populist politics the scope of mass privatization was reduced.

All in all, I have believed all the time that the performance of the Polish economy would have been even better if the SOE's privatization were faster, which had required and early introduction of some scheme of mass privatization.

*

The radical economic program was worked out and implemented during the period of extraordinary politics, which

---

[69] He was a co-author in 1988 of the concept of the voucher privatization (Lewandowski, 1989).

lasted up to the spring 1991. We used it by moving fast which in turn was made possible thanks to the existence of the competent and cohesive team and to the special mechanisms of coordination. There had been relatively little criticism from the politicians and the media. However, the economic establishment was non-supportive or critical. With the passage of time the criticism and protests from the politicians and the interest groups got stronger, especially in 1991.

I focused on policies and dedicated little time to explaining them to the public. I believed this was the best use I could make of the short period of 'extraordinary politics'

7. HONG KONG: THE ONGOING ECONOMIC MIRACLE

By Jean-François Minardi

We could say that the bulk part of countries ranked as most free of the world have a common characteristic, they suffered what Venezuela is suffering, socialism, communism and cronyism. Nevertheless, with real free-market oriented policies those countries have overcame their weaknesses and now are some of the most prosperous in the world. Hong Kong is one of those countries, despite the political regime ruling China, the maintanence of its free market institutions has been the fundamental rock where its long-run prosperity is build. When I read Jean-François Minardi's Economic Note, from the Montreal Economic Institute, I linked directly with Venezuela's situation. One of my most disseminated lectures is Venezuela from Riches to Rags, now it is time to let Minardi explains how Hong Kong went from Rags to Riches...

Hong Kong today is a doorway to China and the rest of Asia for foreign investors, and one of the wealthiest societies in the world. Its gross domestic product per capita is even higher than Britain's[70]. And yet, after the Second World War, this minuscule territory of the British Empire, devoid of natural resources, was faced with the problems of a developing country, with a rapidly expanding poor population. In 1960, the average income per capita was still just 28% of what residents of the far-off mother country earned at the time. What explains this economic miracle and the continuing dynamism of Hong Kong's economy?

---

[70] Hong Kong's gross domestic product per capita at purchasing power parity is 40% higher than Britain's (US$52,830 compared to US$37,860).

From Rags to Riches

When the Japanese occupation ended in 1945, Hong Kong's economy was completely devastated. Furthermore, with the establishment of an embargo on trade with China in 1951 during the Korean War, Hong Kong was no longer in a position to maintain the entrepot trade upon which a large portion of its traditional economic activity was based[71].

The territory nonetheless managed to meet this challenge by finding new sources of development that were at the root of its industrial takeoff in the 1950s. It generally benefited from the arrival of hundreds of thousands of refugees fleeing the civil war and searching for employment, and also from entrepreneurs, knowledge and capital from Shanghai, the great capitalist Chinese city of the day.

Hong Kong's entrepreneurs created an impressive number of small and medium-sized businesses during this period, especially in the textile sector. These SMBs, which gradually branched out into garments, electronics and plastics, were essentially producing to meet the growing demand for affordable manufactured goods in North America and Europe. Their success was remarkable and exports grew from 54% of GDP in the 1960s to 64% in the 1970s.

The rapid industrialization of the 1950s is due to conditions in which property rights were protected, the judiciary power was independent and the courts impartial, and there was a minimum of interference on the part of the colonial authorities when it came to international trade.

Moreover, while the United Kingdom was setting up a highly interventionist welfare state at home, the territory enjoyed a fundamentally free-market economic policy personified by Sir John Cowperthwaite, Financial Secretary of Hong Kong from

---

[71] Entrepot trade is a trade that rests on the importation and re-exportation of goods sheltered from the collection of tariffs or taxes.

1961 to 1971. Despite opposition from London, but with the support of the local business community, Cowperthwaite banked on free trade, the non-intervention of the state in the economy, a strict budgetary policy, a flat personal income tax of 15% and a flexible labour market.

This economic policy, which promoted competition and a spirit of enterprise, created the conditions for very rapid economic growth. It is during this time that Hong Kong became one of the four Asian Tigers, along with Singapore, South Korea and Taiwan.

Between 1961 and 2009, Hong Kong's real GDP per capita was multiplied by a factor of nine. Today, its GDP per capita at purchasing power parity is the 13th highest in the world. Hong Kong therefore succeeded, in just a few decades, in transforming its economy into one of the wealthiest in the world.

From Manufacturing Economy to a Service Economy

The first stage of Hong Kong's development had relied on the manufacturing industry. Mainland China's economic reforms and the policy of openness to foreign investment put in place by Deng Xiaoping starting in 1978 profoundly changed the nature of Hong Kong's economy in the ensuing years.

Hong Kong's manufacturing sector began to decline in the late 1970s due to increases in the price of land and rising salaries. However, Hong Kong's increased economic integration with mainland China allowed it to relocate its production to the special economic zones in the bordering province of Guangdong.

These zones, which were set up beginning in 1980, offered Hong Kong investors the opportunity to enhance their competitiveness by relying on plentiful low-cost labour, while still enjoying the same non-interventionist conditions from the Chinese government as they did in Hong Kong. From 1978 to 1997, trade between Hong Kong and the People's Republic of China grew at an average yearly rate of 28%. By the end of 1997,

59

direct investment from Hong Kong accounted for 80% of all foreign direct investment in Guangdong.

These new developments altered Hong Kong's economy significantly. Industry's share of the economy declined from 31% in 1980 to 14% in 1997 and 8% in 2008; the service sector, on the other hand, increased its share considerably, from 68% in 1980 to 86% in 1997 and 92% in 2008.

Since 1997, Hong Kong's economy has become a centre for high value-added services (finance, management, logistics, business consulting, trade, etc.), as much for Chinese businesses seeking to break into international markets as for businesses around the world looking for access to the markets of mainland China and the rest of Asia.

The Maintenance of Free-Market Institutions

From the early 1980s, the perspective of an impending return of Hong Kong to Chinese sovereignty produced great uncertainty with regard to the maintenance of the institutions that had made the territory wealthy. This concern, however, was quickly appeased.

In the Sino-British Joint Declaration, signed on December 19, 1984, it was established that Hong Kong would cease to be a territory under British control on July 1, 1997. The "one country, two systems" principle was also agreed upon at this time. Excepting foreign affairs and national defense, it grants broad autonomy to the territory and allows it to retain its capitalist system as well as its way of living for a period of 50 years, until the year 2047.

Hong Kong is now a Special Administrative Region of the People's Republic of China that has preserved the bulk of the political, judicial, economic and financial system that characterized the colony when it was in the British fold. The judicial power is independent of the political power and continues to operate under the common law system inherited from the British. Property rights are guaranteed by the Basic Law, which today serves as the constitution of the Hong Kong Special Administrative Region, and the citizens enjoy fundamental individual liberties.

According to the Fraser Institute's Economic Freedom of the World index, Hong Kong's economy has been the freest in the world since 1970. This economic freedom rests on three elements:

1. Smaller Government

Government spending as a percentage of GDP is just 19.2% in Hong Kong, compared to 42.9% in Canada. Personal income tax is a flat 15% and the corporate tax rate is set at 16.5%. It should be noted also that there is no sales tax, and no tax on dividends or capital gains.

2. Flexible, efficient regulation of economic activity

Hong Kong is the second easiest place in the world to conduct business, according the World Bank's Doing Business report, which measures the cost of business regulation for companies each year. Hong Kong has always had a flexible labour market, although in 2011, the legislature adopted, for the first time in its history, a minimum wage law. Finally, the Hong Kong dollar is a stable, fully convertible currency.

3. Openness to international trade

Hong Kong charges no customs duties and imposes no quotas. The bulk of trade in goods takes place with mainland China, which accounted for 54.1% of the total value of exports in 2012, as well as 47.1% of imports. There are no restrictions on the entry or repatriation of capital either, nor on the conversion and transfer of profits and dividends from direct investment. This explains why Hong Kong ranked third in the world after the United States and mainland China in terms of inflow of foreign direct investment in 2012, and fourth after the

United States, Japan and mainland China in terms of outflow.

The free flow of capital has helped make Hong Kong an international financial centre of the first order. In September 2012, the Hong Kong Stock Exchange was the sixth largest in the world and second largest in Asia in terms of market capitalization. According to the Global Financial Centres Index, Hong Kong is also the most competitive financial centre in Asia and the third most competitive in the world behind only London and New York.

The rules of the game are fair for all investors, whether or not they are residents of Hong Kong. There are no restrictions on foreign ownership; foreigners can invest in local businesses and hold up to 100% of capital[72]. Intellectual property is protected, and Hong Kong is one of the least corrupt societies in the world[73].

Access for foreign investors is facilitated by the fact that in 2003, Hong Kong signed a Closer Economic Partnership Agreement (CEPA) with mainland China. Now, practically all goods and services produced in Hong Kong can enter mainland China's market without paying customs duties. Importantly, foreign companies can enjoy these same conditions by outsourcing their activities or by setting up a joint venture with a Hong Kong firm.

---

[72] With the exception of crown corporations as well as broadcasting and cable television, where foreign ownership cannot exceed 49%.

[73] Hong Kong is ranked 14th by Transparency International's 2012 Corruption Perceptions Index, ahead of countries like Japan, the United Kingdom, the United States and France.

Conclusion

Hong Kong is one of the most striking and conclusive examples in the world of a society that succeeded in escaping underdevelopment by relying on economic freedom. With the transition to Chinese sovereignty, Hong Kong preserved the bulk of its liberties and maintained the dynamism of its economy. The future prosperity of the territory will depend largely on the preservation of the free-market institutions and the maintenance of the economic policies that have served it so well to this day.

8. NEW ZEALAND: HOW FREEDOM WORKS
By Daniel Mitchell

*Dan Mitchell is Chairman of the Center for Freedom
and Prosperity. In this chapter, I included two of his
articles about New Zealand. This country is another
great example of how economic freedom reforms
work. Venezuela requires a government that promotes
drastic pro free market reforms -not an increment of
public debt and expenditure-, that incentives and does
not intervene in the creation of wealth by the citizens,
otherwise Venezuela will never overcome the Socialist
trap.*

Тhe Unsung Economic Success Story of New Zealand:

When writing newly updated numbers from
Economic Freedom of the World, I mentioned in passing
that New Zealand deserves praise "for big reforms in the right
direction." And when I say big reforms, this isn't exaggeration
or puffery.

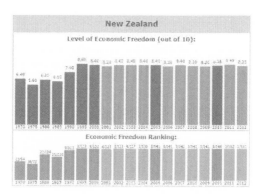

Back in 1975, New Zealand's score from EFW was only 5.60.
To put that in perspective, Greece's score today is 6.93 and
France is at 7.30. In other words, New Zealand was a statist
basket cast 40 years ago, with a degree of economic liberty akin

to where Ethiopia is today and below the scores we now see in economically unfree nations such as Ukraine and Pakistan.

But then policy began to move in the right direction, especially between 1985 and 1995, the country became a Mecca for market-oriented reforms. The net result is that New Zealand's score dramatically improved and it is now comfortably ensconced in the top-5 for economic freedom, usually trailing only Hong Kong and Singapore.

To appreciate what's happened in New Zealand, let's look at excerpts from a 2004 speech by Maurice McTigue, who served in the New Zealand parliament and held several ministerial positions.

He starts with a description of the dire situation that existed prior to the big wave of reform.

New Zealand's per capita income in the period prior to the late 1950s was right around number three in the world, behind the United States and Canada. But by 1984, its per capita income had sunk to 27th in the world, alongside Portugal and Turkey. Not only that, but our unemployment rate was 11.6 percent, we'd had 23 successive years of deficits (sometimes ranging as high as 40 percent of GDP), our debt had grown to 65 percent of GDP, and our credit ratings were continually being downgraded. Government spending was a full 44 percent of GDP, investment capital was exiting in huge quantities, and government controls and micromanagement were pervasive at every level of the economy. We had foreign exchange controls that meant I couldn't buy a subscription to The Economist magazine without the permission of the Minister of Finance. I couldn't buy shares in a foreign company without surrendering my citizenship. There were price controls on all goods and services, on all shops and on all service industries. There were wage controls and wage freezes. I couldn't pay my employees more—or pay them bonuses—if I wanted to. There were import controls on the goods that I could bring into the country. There were massive levels of subsidies on industries in order to keep

65

them viable. Young people were leaving in droves.

Maurice then discusses the various market-oriented reforms that took place, including spending restraint.

What's especially impressive is that New Zealand dramatically shrank government bureaucracies.

When we started this process with the Department of Transportation, it had 5,600 employees. When we finished, it had 53. When we started with the Forest Service, it had 17,000 employees. When we finished, it had 17. When we applied it to the Ministry of Works, it had 28,000 employees. I used to be Minister of Works, and ended up being the only employee. ...if you say to me, "But you killed all those jobs!"—well, that's just not true. The government stopped employing people in those jobs, but the need for the jobs didn't disappear. I visited some of the forestry workers some months after they'd lost their government jobs, and they were quite happy. They told me that they were now earning about three times what they used to earn—on top of which, they were surprised to learn that they could do about 60 percent more than they used to!

And there was lots of privatization.
...we sold off telecommunications, airlines, irrigation schemes, computing services, government printing offices, insurance companies, banks, securities, mortgages, railways, bus services, hotels, shipping lines, agricultural advisory services, etc. In the main, when we sold those things off, their productivity went up and the cost of their services went down, translating into major gains for the economy. Furthermore, we decided that other agencies should be run as profit-making and tax-paying enterprises by government. For instance, the air traffic control system was made into a stand-alone company, given instructions that it had to make an acceptable rate of return and pay taxes, and told that it couldn't get any investment capital from its owner (the government). We did that with about 35 agencies. Together, these used to cost us about one billion dollars per year; now they produced about one billion dollars

per year in revenues and taxes.

Equally impressive, New Zealand got rid of all farm subsidies...and got excellent results.

...as we took government support away from industry, it was widely predicted that there would be a massive exodus of people. But that didn't happen. To give you one example, we lost only about three-quarters of one percent of the farming enterprises— and these were people who shouldn't have been farming in the first place. In addition, some predicted a major move towards corporate as opposed to family farming. But we've seen exactly the reverse. Corporate farming moved out and family farming expanded.

Maurice also has a great segment on education reform, which included school choice.

But since I'm a fiscal policy wonk, I want to highlight this excerpt on the tax reforms.

We lowered the high income tax rate from 66 to 33 percent, and set that flat rate for high-income earners. In addition, we brought the low end down from 38 to 19 percent, which became the flat rate for low-income earners. We then set a consumption tax rate of 10 percent and eliminated all other taxes—capital gains taxes, property taxes, etc. We carefully designed this system to produce exactly the same revenue as we were getting before and presented it to the public as a zero sum game. But what actually happened was that we received 20 percent more revenue than before. Why? We hadn't allowed for the increase in voluntary compliance.

And I assume revenue also climbed because of Laffer Curve-type economic feedback. When more people hold jobs and earn higher incomes, the government gets a slice of that additional income.

Let's wrap this up with a look at what New Zealand has done

to constrain the burden of government spending. If you review my table of Golden Rule success stories, you'll see that the nation got great results with a five-year spending freeze in the early 1990s. Government shrank substantially as a share of GDP.

Nation	Years	Average Annual Spending Growth	Change in burden of Government/GDP	Change in Deficit/GDP
Ireland	1985-1989	1.5%	-12.2%	-9.9%
New Zealand	1991-1997	0.5%	-11.0%	-5.8%
Sweden	1992-2001	1.9%	-15.0%	-10.5%
Canada	1992-1997	0.8%	-9.4%	-9.3%
Netherlands	1995-2000	1.5%	-5.2%	-3.8%
Italy	1996-2000	1.1%	-6.2%	-6.0%
Singapore	1998-2007	-1.1%	-15.9%	-10.4%
Slovakia	2000-2004	1.3%	-14.5%	-9.9%
Taiwan	2001-2006	-0.6%	-5.9%	-7.0%
Israel	2002-2005	0.8%	-5.7%	-2.7%
Germany	2003-2007	0.2%	-5.4%	-4.3%
Switzerland	2004-Present	1.9%	-3.2%	-1.4%
Estonia	2008-2011	1.1%	-5.4%	-4.3%
Lithuania	2008-2012	0.8%	+1.3%	-0.4%
Latvia	2008-Present	-4.2%	-7.1%	-7.0%
Iceland	2009-Present	1.9%	-6.7%	-6.8%

Source: IMF World Economic Outlook database, spending at all levels of government.

Then, for many years, the spending burden was relatively stable as a share of economic output, before then climbing when the recession hit at the end of last decade.

But look at what's happened since then. The New Zealand government has imposed genuine spending restraint, with outlays climbing by an average of 1.88 percent annually according to IMF data. And because that complies with my Golden Rule (meaning that government spending is growing slower than the private sector), the net result according to OECD data is that the burden of government spending is shrinking relative to the size of the economy's productive sector.

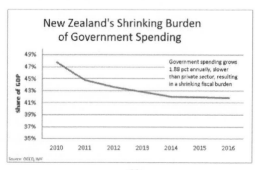

68

New Zealand's Road Map for Sweeping Pro-Market Reform

New Zealand doesn't rank above Hong Kong and Singapore, which routinely rank as the two jurisdictions with the most economic liberty. But it deserves praise for rising so far and fast considering how the country was mired in statist misery just three decades ago. New Zealand made a radical shift to free markets in key areas such as agriculture, trade, fisheries, and industry.

New Zealand's shift to a property rights-based fisheries system is a remarkable success. But I'm even more impressed that the country, which has a very significant agricultural sector, decided to eliminate all subsidies. I fantasize about similar reforms in the United States.

To give you an idea of New Zealand's overall deregulatory success, it is now ranked first in the World Bank's Doing Business.

As a fiscal policy wonk, I like the reforms to tax and budget policy.

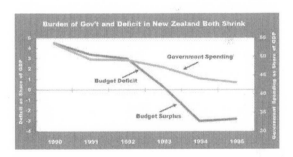

There's a very positive story to tell. In the early 1990s, the government basically imposed a nominal spending freeze. And during that five-year period, the burden of government spending fell by more than 10-percentage points of GDP.

And because policy makers dealt with the underlying disease of too much spending, that also meant eliminating the symptom

69

of red ink. In other words, a big deficit became a big surplus.

The same thing also has been happening this decade. Outlays have been increasing by an average of less than 2 percent annually. And because this complies with my Golden Rule, that means a shrinking burden of spending.

And there's also a good story to tell about tax policy. The top income tax rate has been slashed from 66 percent to 33 percent, and the capital gains tax has been abolished.

Let's close by highlighting what should be the main lesson from New Zealand, namely that any country can rescue itself from economic decline.

New Zealand's reforms are – or at least should be – a road map for Venezuela to follow. The Fraser Institute's Economic Freedom of the World shows the history of economic liberty in the two nations, and you can see that Venezuela used to be a little better than New Zealand between 1970 and to 1980. But then New Zealand jumped ahead, both because policy improved in New Zealand and because it got even worse in Venezuela.

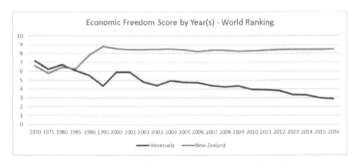

Policy has been generally stable in New Zealand this century. That's acceptable since the country enjoys a high degree of economic liberty. Venezuela, by contrast, has suffered a slow and steady decline. That's basically a recipe for continued misery in the country. But the good news is that Venezuela can simply copy New Zealand to get the same good results.

9. GEORGIAN ECONOMIC REFORMS: THE REST OF THE STORY

By Larisa Burakova & Robert Lawson

Georgia is other example of how economic freedom reforms can change a post-communist country to one of the freest and prosperous countries of the world. ¿Can be applied Bendukidze's reforms in Venezuela?, ¿Who could be the Venezuelan with the Bendukidze's commitment?, ¿The socialism and cronyism in the Venezuela's politicians, media and some "businessmen" would allow these reforms?, Venezuelans might answer those questions. While, Professors Burakova and Lawson explain the Economic Reforms of Georgia and let us know the greatness of freedom. This is an authorized short version of one chapter of their book "Georgia's Rose Revolution. How one country beat the odds, transformed its economy and provided a model for reformers everywhere" published by The Antigua Forum of Universidad Francisco Marroquín. Larisa Burakova is an economist at the institute of Economic Analysis in Moscow. Robert A. Lawson is professor at Southern Methodist University's Cox School of Business; he is co-author of the Economic Freedom of the World annual report, he and Benjamin Powell authored the book "Socialism Sucks: Two economists drink their way through the unfree world".

The Georgian reforms were inspired by idea creators such as Adam Smith, Ludwig von Mises, Friedrich Hayek, and Milton Friedman. Their ideas were picked up and popularized by intellectuals (traders in ideas), including journalists and policy analysts (such as those at Cato Institute, Mises Institute, Institute for Economic Affairs).

But ideas, though absolutely necessary, will not spontaneously create reforms. It takes real men and women of action to implement the idea of economic freedom.

Into this role stepped Mikheil Saakashvili, a Columbia University-educated, smooth-talking politician, who emerged as the nation's leader after the Rose Revolution in 2003. Saakashvili appointed key players, including Vano Merabishvili in the Ministry of Internal Affairs and Zurab Adeishvili in the Ministry of Justice, to whom he gave power in the form of the opportunity and the freedom to implement their ideas.

While the role of Saakashvili is critical to the story, the central hero of Georgia's economic reforms is another man of action: Kakha Bendukidze. A Georgian native and businessman, Bendukidze made a fortune in post-Soviet Russia.

During his visit to Georgia, Bendukidze was invited to meet President Saakashvili and share his views on economic reform. The president asked him what skills were needed for a minister of economy. Bendukidze simply answered, "The main thing you need is someone who understands the meaning of freedom." By the end of the meeting he had been offered the job of Georgia's minister of economy.

Most of Georgia's economic reforms can be classified into three broad categories: de-bureaucratization, privatization, and liberalization.

De-Bureaucratization

Bendukidze and his team believed their government was bloated with too many employees doing too little work. They responded with a systematic review of executive branch jobs in early 2004, which resulted in huge personnel cuts.

The fact that only the deputy and bookkeeper were present at the Price Inspection Office, and of sixty Antimonopoly Service employees no more than fifteen were around, served as eloquent proof that the entities were superfluous. In August 2004 the Price Inspection and Antimonopoly Service were eliminated. In their place, about one year later, the Agency for Free Trade and Competition was created, with a staff of six.

The personnel cuts were huge. In the Ministry of Agriculture, the number of employees went from 4,374 to 600; in Tbilisi City Hall, from 2,500 to 800; in the Ministry of Environment Protection, from more than 5,000 to just 1,700. Similarly, the number of government ministries fell from eighteen to thirteen.

Prior to this reform, the Ministries of Internal Affairs and State Security employed seventy-five thousand people. In December 2004, the two ministries were merged into a new Ministry of Internal Affairs (MIA). Each department and service was reviewed to exclude duplicate functions. The new MIA had twenty-seven thousand employees, a nearly two-thirds reduction in total staff.

Georgian authorities chose a radical method of reforming the police structures which were not working. The first clear demonstration of this approach was with the traffic police. The State Traffic Inspection was one of the most corrupt units in the Georgian government.

The reform was headed by Vano Merabishvili, the minister of internal affairs and an ally of Bendukidze. In early summer of 2004, Merabishvili eliminated the State Traffic Inspection, firing all fifteen thousand employees in a single day! Two months later, in August 2004, the force was replaced by competitive hiring of employees for the newly formed US-style highway patrol. During the two-month transition period there was no policing of the roads, and yet the number of car accidents did not increase. There were no riots and no attempts to preserve the status quo by former employees.

The lesson is clear: abolishing a nonfunctioning institution that lived off extortion had no negative consequences; instead it cleared the way for a better institution to emerge.

Privatization

Privatization began immediately after independence in 1992, although a comprehensive privatization process did not begin fully until 2004 under Bendukidze. Today most large-scale state properties have been privatized, and privatization of small- and medium-sized properties and enterprises is ongoing. Bendukidze himself coined the catchphrase for the Georgian privatization program: "Everything is for sale, except honor"[74].

Initially the idea to privatize so-called "strategic assets" was not widely accepted among government officials or the general public. With Bendukidze's leadership, that attitude quickly changed.

Under Bendukidze's leadership, Georgia's privatization programs were among the most extensive and least corrupt in the former Soviet Union. The strategy was simple: auction off state assets to the highest bidder, frequently without any conditions, with the funds going to the state. By all accounts the auctions were open to everyone, with no preference given to Georgians over foreigners. Even Russians could participate, despite worries about threats to territorial integrity or the possible danger caused by selling strategic assets to other countries.

The Georgian approach of transparent auctions of state-owned assets stands in contrast to the privatizations in other post-Soviet countries. In the latter, many times assets were simply sold at very low prices to political cronies or to the political leaders themselves. In other cases, citizens were given vouchers with which they could buy stock in newly privatized companies. The reality, however, was that many people did not recognize the value of the vouchers and were eager to sell them cheaply, even bartering them for food or liquor. Many people felt that unscrupulous brokers had cheated them out of their vouchers. The unfortunate side effect was that privatization specifically, and capitalism more generally, became linked in people's minds

---

[74] N.A.: The English translation is not as precise as it could be.

with corruption and fraud.

An excellent example of how well the process worked is the privatization of the Intourist Hotel, the first property to be sold under Bendukidze's new plan. This highly desirable hotel was located in the Black Sea resort town of Batumi. The challenges began with the first potential buyer, who appeared almost immediately. He was a local crony who offered 150,000 lari (about $80,000). Bendukidze's project manager replied, "No. We are going to sell the hotel at auction and we expect it to be sold for at least three million US dollars." The buyer increased his offer to 500,000 lari, but the decision had been made to carry out an open auction, with bids starting at three million dollars.

The crony did everything he could to disrupt the auction and scare away potential bidders, including spreading rumors that the bidding was already rigged in his favor. In the end, a Siberian businessman with Georgian roots and fond memories of the location from his youth was identified by Bendukidze's agent and encouraged to participate in the auction. He won the bidding with a final price of $3.02 million.

Another key principle of Bendukidze's privatization plan was that there would be no conditions on the sale of assets. The properties were to be sold as is, and the new owners would be free to do with them as they pleased. This principle was frequently tested, however, when it came to so-called "strategic" assets. The political reality was that many large privatizations required conditions. The challenge was to adopt conditions that satisfied these political realities but did not interfere substantially with market realities so that the assets ended up in the hands of those who valued them most highly.

The privatizations went well beyond the largest state-held assets such as hotels and power plants. On a smaller scale, but no less politically sensitive, was the issue of state-held farmland. Here, privatization would present both an opportunity and a challenge.

A key compromise was adopted to assuage fears and make privatization work politically, while retaining the key principle of selling off state assets as efficiently as possible. During the early stages of the draft law, it was decided that certain farmland auctions would be open only to residents of neighboring villages. These were for parcels that had been rented from the government, about 35 percent of the farmland. In addition, the local residents themselves could decide on the size of each lot (but these could be no less than three hectares, if there was no natural border such as a forest or river). Opening bids were set at twice the annual land tax, and residents could bid this up in competition to acquire land. While this more restrictive approach likely reduced revenue from land auctions, it also reduced political tension and allowed the process to work.

In a few special cases, state assets were privatized with different conditions. Hospitals in particular required special treatment. The reformers wanted to get inefficient state-run hospitals out of the hands of the government. At the same time, whatever rules they established would need to guarantee a certain standard of service. Compromises would have to be made to privatize hospital properties. For example, if an investor was interested in a state hospital building in a commercially attractive location, such as the capital's downtown, he could acquire the property without buying it directly. Instead, the investor would assume the responsibility of building new hospitals in specific areas stipulated in the contract, and guarantee the availability of a minimum number of beds. This allowed the property to be privatized and put to its most valued use while assuring the public that hospitals would still be available. Even though the government's first priority was to generate revenue, it was understood that not all assets could be sold immediately and without conditions.

Liberalization

Private property is the bedrock of a market system. When the freedom to produce, hire and fire, buy and sell, and consume freely is severely restricted, private property is per se not that valuable. True economic freedom requires eliminating the impediments facing people in their business lives. The Georgian economy left over from its days under the Soviet Union was in desperate need of economic liberalization in virtually every sphere of economic life. From paying taxes to hiring workers to opening businesses, red tape and complexity needed to be reduced.

Immediately following the disintegration of the Soviet Union, the income and payroll tax systems were modeled after highincome nations and designed with the help of the International Monetary Fund. The tax system was highly complicated and progressive, and even more ill-suited to a poor, mostly agricultural economy attempting to attract foreign investors. The system was so complex, and so corrupt, that it raised little revenue. Something needed to be done to simplify the tax code, weed out corruption, and get people paying some taxes.

Bendukidze and his reformers set out to radically reshape the tax system. Both the number of taxes and the tax rates were dramatically lowered. The number of distinct taxes was reduced from twenty-two to seven, and later to six. Tax rates were lowered just as notably. Georgia first instituted a 12 percent flat income tax and other reforms such as a relatively simple 18 percent value-added tax (VAT). Three years later, the wage tax used to fund social pensions was eliminated entirely and folded into the flat income tax. This brought the total tax on wages down from 33 percent to 20 percent.

Tax reform was accompanied by amnesty for most taxpayers who owed back taxes under the previously high rates. This measure helped to drum up support for the new system among taxpayers themselves.

In addition to tax policy, another area in need of reform was the labor market. The labor code was a residual of the Soviet-era code from 1973. As such, unionization was essentially required and labor unions enjoyed many special privileges under the law.

Georgia's new labor code is very similar to the English common law "at will" code and only about twenty pages long[75]. The key rule is that employees and employers must honor contractual agreements. They can be individual or collective, but there are no special privileges conferred to unions above and beyond those afforded to individuals. Some regulations exist related to termination notifications, severance pay, leaves, vacation pay, and the like. Frequently, however, the law allows the parties to explicitly contract around these regulations.

Bendukidze's reform team worked closely with the Liberty Institute in drafting the law. The Liberty Institute is a highly respected NGO that was instrumental during the Rose Revolution, and getting them on board was deemed important. The Liberty Institute was mainly interested in nondiscrimination codes, but in the end agreed to the more general idea of simple equality under the law.

The labor reform was one of the few reforms accompanied by tough discussions in the media and parliament. The main strategy of the reformers was to explain the expected outcome of liberalization since the majority of the opposition simply embraced Soviet-style paternalistic logic.

---

[75] See the website of the International Labour Organization

PART 3: GENERAL TREATMENT

10. A SOCIALIST DEMOCRACY: IS IT VIABLE?

By Hugo Faría

A friend of mine says "Hugo Faría is the best classical liberal economist of Venezuela, and has great ideas very close to the Austrian School", I think he is right, and even his Hugo's definition is too small to the great –not only economist- person he is. Faría was professor at IESA and a promoter of real Freedom for Venezuela. Hugo teaches and researches in economics at the University of Miami, and he is the Senior Researcher & Policies Consultant of Econintech. He has published in many journals in United States, his articles covered not only Venezuela's crisis but also economic growth and development, institutions, and economic freedom. Hugo holds a PhD from the University of South Caroline and a Master in Public Policies from University of Chicago. He was a Keynesian-socialist, apologies for the redundancy, after graduating in economics from UCAB in Caracas, but in his PhD studies several professors changed his economic vision, and now he defines himself as an "Austrian-mathematical economist" which he does not perceives as an oxymoron. He focuses his work on the defense of the property rights of the average citizen. In this article, he explains why a socialist-democracy will sooner or later implode, leading to the conclusion that political freedom necessitates economic freedom to persist. If Venezuelans want a real democracy that ensures a long-run prosperity and freedom, they should heed Hugo's suggestions.

I define, following Lenin, socialism as a political/economic institutional arrangement whereby the government is the owner of the commanding heights of the economy. The commanding heights of the economy encompass its most profitable sectors. In the less developed countries, the

79

commanding heights frequently comprise oil, natural gas, steel, and aluminum, as well as coal, gold, diamond and iron mines. According to Lenin, if the government is the owner of the commanding heights, a true communist should not be bothered by the existence of private property in marginal areas of the economy such as agriculture, commerce and industry, all in activities of secondary importance, for example, clothing, beer and assembly lines of cars.

This notion of socialism is somewhat different from the welfare state, whereby the government provides "free" education and health care. For the purpose of this essay, a crucial difference between a socialist arrangement and a welfare state is that the government ownership of the commanding heights could yield a considerable amount of revenues to the government, bypassing citizens. Whereas a welfare state commonly represents a substantial source of expenditures for the government, which at least in the developed world, is financed with taxes levied on the citizenry.

Notwithstanding the aforementioned difference, I should note that socialism and welfare state have in common an unwarranted grab by the government. For starters, education and health care are mainly private goods, that is, rival and excludable. A substantial body of evidence clearly suggests that markets function well in the allocation of scarce resources, in the presence of private goods. Hence, governments supplying education and health care are two examples of governmental overreach. In the case of socialism, it is plain that markets' invisible hand does a much better job managing companies than governments' visible foot. Thus, the welfare state and socialism are cases of unnecessary governmental intrusions.[91] [92]

---

[91] Other potential problems stemming from a welfare state are the perilous dependence of the people on government and the commencement of a slippery slope dynamics which may lead to more unnecessary grabs by government, such as expropriation of companies.
[92] This line of thought does not deny the convenience of government subsidization of education and health care to low income individuals.

Socialism and democracy: Compatible?

I will attempt to answer this question appealing to arguments drawn from three different lines of inquiry. Namely, a) moral philosophy; b) historical evidence and c) modern evidence.

a) Democracy is about political freedom, which presupposes the right to vote in or out of office someone, entails competition among political parties and their representatives. Moreover, checks and balances among the three branches of government implying a broad distribution of power are relevant for the persistence of democracy.

Economic socialism is about the concentration of economic power at the government level. The government is the owner of the most productive sectors of the economy. As such, it prevents free participation of citizens, nationals or foreigners. The board of directors and top-level managers are typically designated by the government, in the style of command and control policy decisions. On the contrary, modern corporations' managerial teams, are elected by shareholders who are risking their capital and therefore are incentivized to elect the best directors and managers in light of existing information.

Thus, democracy is about institutions, rules of the political game, which are inclusive. While economic socialistic institutions are exclusionary. Consequently, no mutual reinforcement emerges between political and economic rules of the game, contributing to impede the arrival of a virtuous circle driven by inclusive economic and political institutions (Acemoglu and Robinson 2012). Accordingly, the different approaches of economic socialism and democracy, strongly suggest that coexistence of those two institutional arrangements are bound to clash inducing high instability which will lead to a

---

The goal is to provide better opportunities to people unable to finance investments in human capital allowing them to overcome their predicament. Procuring the emergence of self-reliant individuals, who do not necessitate governmental aid, is critically important.

81

paltry rate of economic growth.

b) Historical evidence suggests that the onset of lasting democracy is preceded by an impoverished crown. Indeed, in all incipient democracies that emerged in ancient and medieval periods, the state recognized private property rights of the citizens. This is true for the ancient Athenian democracy and for the medieval cities in Northern Italy, Germany, and the Low Countries during the tenth and eleventh centuries of the Common Era (AD). This historical fact has been attributed to the prevalence of non-patrimonial monarchies in Western Europe, which allowed for private property and therefore protection from encroachments by the king (See Pipes 1999, for example).

In the Near and Far East as well as in the easternmost part of Europe, patrimonial regimes prevailed where the king ruled and owned the land along with the subjects. As the classical scholar Moses Finley (1973) observes, "it is impossible to translate the word freedom, eleuthero in Greek and libertas in Latin, or free man, into any ancient Near Eastern language, including Hebrew, or into any Far Eastern language either, for that matter" (p.28). This quote suggests that the word freedom did not arise in regions of the world where the crown was patrimonial. "For ideas do not form in a vacuum: like words which articulate them, they refer to things that matter sufficiently to require a name in order to make it possible to communicate about them" Pipes (1999, p.110).

The signing of the Magna Carta in 1215, generally considered as the first of the English Statutes of the Realm, was provoked by the nobles who took advantage of King John's fiscal predicament. Indeed, King John asked the barons for money after his defeat at the Battle of Bovines in France. The barons, in what will be a classical bargain in English constitutional history, provided the money in exchange for rights. In fact, the content of two salient property related clauses, established in the Great Charter are worth mentioning. The first one contemplated that the king, to raise taxes, had to consult with the barons. The second one established the protection of barons and nobles' private property. Both dispositions contributed to restrain the king's power.[93]

The ensuing four hundred and seventy-three years were marked by a constitutional struggle between the parliament and the crown of epical proportions. William of Orange acknowledged that he is king because this was the will of the English Parliament, sealing the victory of parliament over the crown. Rule of law emerged permanently in the aftermath of the 1688 Glorious Revolution enabling the gradual emergence of parliamentary democracy. Subjecting the king to the law would not have been possible if the crown had not been impoverished and the people, the commoners, had not been enriched.[94] [95]

Conversely, in continental Europe, particularly in France and Spain, absolutism intensified. This was due to the flow of precious metals into the crowns' coffers, stemming from colonial extraction in the case of Spain. In France, the wealth of the crown originated by Royal domain income, which became a major obstacle to subdue the king. To the point that in the fourteenth and fifteenth century the French king was the wealthiest monarch of Europe. These are conspicuous examples of fiscally

---

[93] Evidence suggesting that King John signed the Magna Carta reluctantly, is that after the barons dispersed, the king asked Pope Innocent III to annul it, to which the pope agreed.

[94] This is not to deny the role of fortunate turns of contingency throughout history, such as English naval forces defeating the Spanish Armada in 1588. Thus, the course of history is neither preordained nor inexorable.

[95] Economic historian Gregory Clark (2007) argues that English economic institutions were of high quality since early thirteenth century. "By 1200 societies such as England already had all the institutional prerequisites for economic growth emphasized today by the World Bank and the International Monetary Fund" (p. 10). Clark's observation reinforces the view that economic institutions, which confer private property protections, predate the commencement of modern democratic rule. See also Acemoglu and Robinson (2012) for additional information on the emergence of parliamentary democracy in England.

independent governments suffocating the onset of potential democratization processes.[96]

c) Contemporarily, we find similar cases mirroring historical experiences. On the one hand, the British settler colonies embarking on an institutional trajectory parallel to England's, becoming prosperous democracies. On the other hand, French, Spanish and Portuguese former colonies remain entangled by their colonial legacy. This legacy is marked by a tumultuous morass of extractive economic and political institutions which serve as a formidable obstacle for the establishment of rule of law, sustained economic growth, and political development.

Other modern failures to provide for the dawn of prosperous democracies, are OPEC countries. Their governments are owners of the oil wealth, hindering their chances to establish inclusive economic and political institutions. On the contrary, nations, and regions exhibiting institutional inclusiveness, have dealt with newly found oil wealth efficiently, fostering citizens' welfare. These nations and regions have not endured derailment from neither their sustained prosperous economic paths nor from their high levels of political development. Paradigmatic examples are Norway, England, and Alaska in the United States, let alone Texas.

Another revealing contemporary event is the fracking revolution in the U.S., which has taken place primarily in privately owned land. Thus, who is the owner of the country's

---

[96] In today's Spain during the fourteenth century, the Aragonese oath of allegiance to the king read: "We who are as good as you swear to you who are no better than we, to accept you as our king and sovereign lord, provided you observe all our liberties and laws, but if not, not" Pipes (1999 p.153). This oath was a lot bolder than any oath of allegiance proclaimed in English history. The contrasting political outcomes in England and Spain, Parliamentary Democracy and Absolutism respectively, is a vivid reminder of how fiscal independence of governments can utterly undermine the onset of democracy.

wealth, the state or the people, and how does the state obtain its revenues, taxing the people or through patrimonial rents, seem to matter for the arrival, persistence and flourishing of democracy. An instructive case of failed democracy is Venezuela, one of the fastest growing countries in the world from 1920 to 1957. The onset of social(ist) democracy in 1959 put an end to prosperity and to democracy. The Venezuelan government expropriated foreign oil companies in 1975 and in addition, it already was the owner of the remaining commanding heights of the economy.[97][98]

What to Do in Light of the Evidence?

Based on the preceding brief historical and contemporary accounts, this essay advances the hypothesis that economic freedom is a critical institutional cluster for the emergence and sustainability of democracy. Elevated levels of economic freedom are characterized by limited government, rule of law, trade openness that enriches the population, monetary stability as well as regulations that promote well-functioning markets. These features foster an affluent and vibrant private sector capable of providing a level of tax revenues consistent with intertemporal feasibility of fiscal policy. Under prominent levels of economic freedom, the government lives off the peoples' taxes, it is deprived of fiscal independence and it is financially subjected to the people. This institutional arrangement, characterized by a state that rules but does not own, favors enhanced governmental quality, accountability, and

---

[97] Venezuela's outcome is a stern reminder of Friedman's quote: When a country's leader privilege equality over freedom, the people will end up without freedom and without equality.

[98] Venezuela's growth rate between 1920 and 1957 appears to have been no less than 5% on a per capita basis. The Central Bank of Venezuela estimates an average growth of 5.1% for the 1950-1957 time period. The average growth rate from 1958 to 1980 was 1.18% and between 1981 and 1998, before the advent of Chavez, was minus 2.77%. The average growth rate between 1958 and 1998 was negative 0.27%. Calculations by Acevedo, Cirocco, Faría and Lorca 2018.

transparency; mainstay attributes of thriving democracies.[99]

On the contrary, when governments in modern times are patrimonial, critical natural resources and companies associated with their exploitation, are owned by the state. This ownership may provide a substantial fraction of fiscal revenues. In this case, democracy becomes elusive and even if it arises, chances are that nascent democratic experiments will not last. Accordingly, how the wealth is distributed between the state and the people matters for the onset of democracy and its persistence.[100]

Moreover, the recent comparative economic development literature documents the prominent role of economic freedom igniting long term economic growth. High growth rates are associated with elevated levels of voluntary transactions, spurring an increasingly expanding society of proprietors under the watchful eye of the rule of law. Private property, in turn, induces people to experience self-reliance and the attendant notion of economic freedom.

Ownership of things is concurrently conducive to the idea of ownership of oneself, which leads to the experience of personal freedom. The acquaintance with personal freedom begets the notion of inalienable rights, such as the right to life, liberty, freedom of religion and speech as well as the right to pursue happiness. Not surprisingly, personal freedom leads to political freedoms, formalized in the rights to self-government.

Rule of law is a third potential channel which may spearhead democratization processes and promote democracies' sustainability. Rule of law and its enforcement provides assurances that the will of the electorate will be upheld. The absence of rule of law is a key factor that accounts for the failure

---

[99] Another consequence of patrimonial governments is that the massive amount of power conferred on the state becomes a breeding ground for corruption. As Lord Acton once stated: power corrupts, absolute power corrupts absolutely.

[100] See James Harrington (1656) who originally articulated this notion.

of so many democracies in Latin America.

Equality before the law and one-person-one-vote go together. As English historian Paul Johnson asserts: "Both are needed, but young states find in practice that legal equality, enforced by courts which fear no one, is the substance, formal democracy often the mere shadow."[101]

In sum, this essay contends that economic freedom offers the potential to foster democracy and its persistence relying on three interrelated channels. First, through governmental "starvation", curtailing fiscal independence. Second, by giving rise to a society of proprietors, who through ownership experience personal freedoms which naturally spill-over to the civil and political spheres. Finally, rule of law which is the backbone of democracy. Firmly establishing a judicial system in which everyone in the country is equal before the law, ensures that the wishes of the people, expressed through the voting process, will be enforced.

Specific Reforms

This section summarizes central specific reforms in Venezuela's economy congruous with the notion of raising the level of economic freedom, which I see as a necessary condition for democratic rule and prosperity to persist. The suggested reforms span four fundamental areas of the Venezuelan economy. I) Commanding heights of the economy. II) Institutional monetary arrangement. III) Trade and regulations. IV) The judiciary system. In what follows, this essay provides a brief sketch of the recommended changes in the rules of the game.

I) State-owned companies which belong to the commanding heights of the economy are devolved to Venezuelans. I will briefly focus on the most conspicuous segment, which is the oil sector. Shares of PDVSA, the state-run company, are issued and

---

[101] Paul Johnson (1999).

one share will be transferred to each Venezuelan by birth who is at least 21 years. These shares can be sold. In addition, a package of stocks is sold to international or national investors, with expertise in the oil business. These investors may integrate the managerial team and the board of directors if elected by stockholders. An additional package of stocks should be sold in the open market, listing the company in the Nasdaq Stock Market. Finally, taxes paid by oil companies are deposited in individual bank accounts of Venezuelans by birth older than 21 years of age. This reform is critically important to prevent fiscal independence of the government.

Many issues need to be addressed such as informing citizens on their rights and obligations as stockholders, judicial venues to solve legal conflicts, tax rates applied to oil companies, exiting OPEC, corporate bylaws and chartering, among others. These issues will be examined in a follow-up paper.

II) Monetary freedom, allowing for competition among currencies, including cryptocurrencies and the central bank's currency.

III) Unilateral elimination of trade barriers and regulatory simplification.

IV) Reform of the judicial branch of government, which encompasses its independence, objective adjudication of justice, selection of judges and their qualifications, is one of the most urgent topics. For the vast majority of Latin American countries, the quality of the judiciary system is their weakest area. This reform, of course, will necessarily take more time. In the interim, many legal conflicts of transcendental consequences for the nation can be adjudicated in countries with a reputable judicial track.

Concluding Remarks

A critical check on government is a wealthy population coupled with an impoverished government, whereby government rules but it is not an owner. When governments are owners the tendency is to behave as unconstrained absolutist kings, precluding the emergence of rule of law and consequently of democratic rule. Another consequence of governmental ownership is that the absence of the profit motive is conducive to poorly managed companies. The most profitable sector of the economy in the hands of government is bound to languish, hindering the possibility of the economy reaching its full growth potential. Low growth is also perilous to democracy because it breeds sentiments of redistribution leading to internal conflicts and higher tax rates which exacerbate the exiguous growth. Finally, patrimonial governments are fertile land to scatter the seeds of corruption, which is another growth retarding mechanism.

11. WHY VENEZUELA SHOULD EMBRACE DOLLARIZATION

By Steve Hanke

We must introduce many reforms in Venezuela. Nevertheless, the first objective is to stabilize the economy, and the most reliable and sure way to achieve this objective is by taking away the Government's control of monetary policies. Professor Hanke closely follows Venezuela's economic disaster. Recently, the "Instituto Hanke de Economía Aplicada" in Caracas has been erected in honor of Prof Hanke. He measures Venezuela's inflation daily and with extreme accuracy. Prof. Hanke proposes a dollarization scheme for Venezuela that would bring Venezuela's hyperinflation to a grinding halt, and he promotes Monetary Freedom (see point 5 of Hanke's proposal). When I met Professor Hanke, I immediately understood that Venezuelans can be assured that he is dedicated to providing us a fast, reliable, and infallible solution to stopping Venezuela's hyperinflation that would aid in the rebuilding of our country. As Prof. Hanke often says "Stability might not be everything, but everything is nothing without stability." Steve Hanke is a Professor of Applied Economics at The Johns Hopkins University in Baltimore, Maryland and Senior Fellow and Director of the Trouble Currencies Project at the Cato Institute in Washington, D.C. Hanke served as President Rafael Caldera's advisor from 1994-1995 and is recognized as a leading expert on measuring and stopping hyperinflations.

Venezuela's economy has collapsed. This is the result of years of socialism, incompetence, and corruption, among other things. An important element that mirrors the economy's collapse is Venezuela's currency, the bolívar. It is not trustworthy. Venezuela's exchange rate regime provides no discipline. It only produces instability and poverty. Currently, Venezuela is experiencing one of the highest inflation rates and longest lasting episode of hyperinflation in the world. As of today (Dec. 5, 2018)[102], the episode has lasted 25 months, with today's annual inflation rate at 48,948%.

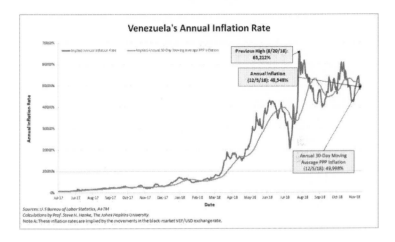

I observed much of Venezuela's economic dysfunction first-hand during the 1995-96 period, when I acted as President Rafael Caldera's adviser. But it wasn't until 1999, when Hugo Chávez was installed as president, that the socialist seeds of Venezuela's current meltdown started to be planted. This is not to say that Venezuela had not suffered from an unstable currency and elevated inflation rates before the arrival of President Chávez, but with his ascendancy, fiscal and monetary discipline further deteriorated and inflation ratcheted up. By the time President Nicolás Maduro arrived in early 2013, annual inflation was in triple digits and rising. Venezuela entered what has become a death spiral.

With the acceleration of inflation, the Banco Central de Venezuela (BCV) became an unreliable source of inflation data.

---

[102] N.E.: On January 1st 2019, Professor Hanke published in Forbes a most updated version and stated that Venezuela's hyperinflation hits 80,000% per year in 2018.

Indeed, in December 2014, the BCV stopped reporting inflation statistics on a regular basis. To remedy this problem, the Johns Hopkins-Cato Institute Troubled Currencies Project, which I direct, began to measure Venezuela's inflation back to 2013[103].

So, how do we accurately measure Venezuela's inflation? There is only one reliable way. The most important price in an economy is the exchange rate between the local currency - in this case, the bolívar - and the world's reserve currency, the U.S. dollar. As long as there is an active black market (read: free market) for currency and the data are available, changes in the black market exchange rate can be reliably transformed into accurate measurements of countrywide inflation rates. The economic principle of purchasing power parity (PPP) allows for this transformation. And the application of PPP to measure elevated inflation rates is rather simple.

Beyond the theory of PPP, the intuition of why PPP represents the 'gold standard' for measuring inflation during hyperinflation episodes is clear. All items in an economy that is hyperinflating are either priced in a stable foreign currency (the U.S. dollar) or a local currency (the bolívar). If goods are priced in terms of bolivars, those prices are determined by referring to the dollar prices of goods, and then converting them to local bolívar prices after checking with the spot black-market exchange rate. Indeed, when the price level is increasing rapidly and erratically on a day-by-day, hour-by-hour, or even minute by-minute basis, exchange rate quotations are the only source of information on how fast inflation is actually proceeding. That is why PPP holds, and why we can use high-frequency (daily) data to calculate Venezuela's inflation rate, even during episodes of hyperinflation.

And what criteria are used to categorize an inflation as an episode of hyperinflation? The following criteria should be met before any episode of elevated inflation be termed "hyperinflation":

---

[103] See Hanke (2016, 2017a, 2017b)

- An episode of hyperinflation occurs when the monthly inflation rate exceeds 50%/mo. for 30 consecutive days.

- The hyperinflation episode ends when the monthly inflation rate falls below 50%/mo. mark, unless the monthly inflation should exceed 50% per month for another 30-day period within a year after the first episode is terminated. In this case, the second episode is not counted as a new hyperinflation episode, but is instead considered a continuation of the original episode.

In Venezuela, the monthly inflation rate exceeded 50%/mo back on November 13, 2016 and remained above 50%/mo until December 14, 2016 (32 consecutive days). On December 15, 2016, the monthly inflation rate fell below 50%/mo mark. Then, on November 3, 2017, the monthly inflation rate again exceeded 50%/mo threshold, before falling below the threshold on December 17, 2017 (for 44 consecutive days). So, Venezuela has been engulfed in a hyperinflation episode ever since November 13, 2016, with another flare up of the same episode occurring during the November-December 2017 period.

How can Venezuela pull itself out of its economic death spiral? Venezuela must officially dump the bolívar and adopt the greenback. Official "dollarization" is a proven elixir. I know because I operated as a State Counselor in Montenegro when it dumped the worthless Yugoslav dinar in 1999 and replaced it with the Deutsche mark. I also took part in the successful dollarization of Ecuador in 2001, when I was operating as an adviser to the Minister of Economy and Finance.

Countries that are officially dollarized produce lower, less variable inflation rates and higher, more stable economic growth rates than comparable countries with central banks that issue domestic currencies. There is a tried and true way to stabilize the economy, which is a necessary condition required before the massive task of life-giving reforms can begin. It is dollarization. Stability might not be everything, but everything is nothing without stability.

Just what does the Venezuelan public think of the dollarization idea? To answer that question, a professional survey of public opinion on the topic was conducted in March 2017 by Datincorp in Caracas. The results are encouraging: Sixty-two (62%) of the public favored dollarization. Since things have considerably deteriorated since that survey, my conjecture is that the proportion of Venezuelans favoring dollarization has substantially increased. It's time for enlightened, practical politicians in Venezuela to embrace the dollarization idea. The fact of the matter is that the public has already spontaneously dollarized the economy.

But, the question I am repeatedly asked is, how do you officially dollarize a place like Venezuela? To do that you need a dollarization law. I have drafted such a model law. The model statute is meant to suggest the main features that are desirable for a law on dollarization. Legal technicalities may require an actual statute to be somewhat different.

A Model Dollarization Statute For Venezuela

1. The Banco Central de Venezuela (BCV) shall cease to issue Venezuelan bolivars expect as replacements for equal amounts of old currency that may become worn out.

2. Except as specified in paragraph 3, wages, prices, assets, and liabilities shall be converted from Venezuelan bolivars to U.S. dollars ("the replacement currency") at the conversion rate chosen in the law that accompanies this law. By 60 days after this law enters into force, wages and prices shall cease to be quoted in Venezuelan bolivars.

3a. Interest rates shall be converted into the replacement currency by the following procedure. The independent committee of experts specified in the law accompanying this law shall choose benchmark interest rates in the Venezuelan bolívar and replacement currency, having similar characteristics with respect to maturity and liquidity insofar as possible. The ratio between existing interest rates in Venezuelan bolivars and the benchmark interest rate in the Venezuelan bolívar shall determine the interest rate in the replacement currency, which shall bear the same ratio to the benchmark rate in the replacement currency.

3b. In no case, however, shall new interest rates in the replacement currency resulting from the conversion procedure exceed 50 percent a year.

4. The president may appoint a committee of experts on technical issues connected with this law to recommend changes in regulations that may be necessary.

5. Nothing in this law shall prevent parties to a transaction from using any currency that is mutually agreeable. However, the replacement currency may be established as the default currency where no other currency is specified.

6. While Venezuelan bolivars remain in circulation, the government shall accept them in payment of taxes at no premium to the conversion rate with the replacement currency. Acceptance of Venezuelan bolivars shall not be obligatory for any other party.

7. Within five years after this law takes effect the government shall redeem all outstanding Venezuelan bolivars for the replacement currency or exchange it for government debt bearing a market-determined rate of interest.

8. Existing laws that conflict with this law are void.

9. This law takes effect immediately upon publication.

12. HOW TO DESOCIALIZE ENTERPRISES: A PRIVATIZATION PROGRAM FOR VENEZUELA

By Rafael Acevedo[104]

In a post-communist and post-socialist Venezuela with sustainable freedom, there is no possibility of state ownership of any enterprise. I want to remark that this is one of the vast differences between Econintech and its members with other groups of Venezuelan professionals and politicians; we do not believe or trust in governments managing natural resources, let alone the commanding heights of the economy. My team has developed a privatization program inspired by previous experiences and following the Austrian School ideals. Venezuelans will have to decide between following the mainstream proposals or opening the doors, following our plans, to long-run Prosperity & Liberty.

Venezuela (circa March 2019) is part of the most commented news around the world. Many countries are leading efforts to help Venezuelans recover freedom. Nonetheless, this attempt seems to focus just on the "political freedom" arena, because the recovery of "democracy" is apparently the unique objective. Sadly, Venezuela has experienced that only democracy is not enough for a long-run prosperity. Indeed, Venezuelans enjoyed such political system for more than 40 years, but rooted in an omnipotent state, overwhelmingly independent of its citizens and considered the "big dad"[105]. In the view of Econintech's team, this has been the main cause of the progressive deterioration leading to the current tyranny, cause that will continue even in the case of a potential

---

[104] I thank Professor Robert Murphy, from the Free Market Institute and Senior Fellow of the Mises Institute, for his comments and suggestions on this essay.

[105] Acevedo & Cirocco in Chapter 5 in this book explain better this comment.

change of the rulers.

Considering this I developed and published a privatization plan for Venezuela's state-controlled enterprises and assets, originally published on the blog of the The Independent Institute and on the website of Econintech, which encompasses minimum state intervention, the impossibility for the government to vote, seventy per cent of the shares delivered to Venezuelans, special conditions for the expropriated people, certain limitations on the percentage of shares owned, and a particular restriction of three years on selling or transferring shares for all Venezuelan who previously received them as part of the process. After that, Econintech's team has been working on the improvement of my previous essay. Now, this essay is the most updated resume about our paper "Desocialization of Enterprises: Empowering Venezuelans" that I presented in the Austrian Economics Research Conference at the Mises Institute in Auburn Alabama, March 2019.

Who is the owner?

Venezuelans have become accustomed to the view whereby oil (and all natural resources) belong to the citizens. The mercantilist and socialist media has disseminated and instilled this false idea. The educational system also espouses this false narrative. However, Venezuelans have neither received the proceeds from oil extraction, taxes and dividends nor have been allowed to have equity shares in the business. On the contrary, because Petróleos de Venezuela Sociedad Anónima (PDVSA, Venezuela's oil company) is a state-owned company, governments are the only direct recipients of those benefits, which confer upon them tremendous economic power and considerable independence from Venezuelan taxpayers.

State-ownership of the commanding heights of the economy is not an original policy created in the Chávez-Maduro regime, but an exclusionary economic institution is resulting from an increasingly powerful combination of democratic socialism and mercantilism implemented by elites in power decades before the

97

advent of Chávez (Faría & Filardo, 2015). With such a tremendous economic power concentrated in the hands of political and economic elites, representatives of "the revolution or socialism of the 21st century" have been able to promote a varied array of destabilizing activities abroad and increment their power hold in the country which has morphed into an internationally recognized tyranny. Hence the prescience of Mises' wisdom:

> If control of production is shifted from the hands of entrepreneurs, daily anew elected by a plebiscite of the consumers into the hands of the supreme commander of the 'industrial armies' or of the 'armed workers', neither representative government nor any civil liberties can survive. (Mises, 2008).

Skepticism on the capacities of Venezuelans

Politicians and certain scholars believe and disseminate that Venezuelans are not capable of handling their own freedom and wealth accurately. It is essential to understand the origin of that stance because when we publicly state our proposal on the effective distribution of shares among all Venezuelan citizens by birth, aged eighteen years or older, we have faced hard skepticism, based upon an alleged lack of knowledge or ability of the average people.

Such underestimation is widespread and, even, not only an exclusive characteristic of politicians and other elites. On social media, the lack of trust in how beneficiaries would manage their shares is commonly expressed. The populist rhetoric, implemented since 1958[106], has instilled a strong bias, to the point that there are people who do not believe in the power of right incentives and individual freedom but do believe in bureaucrats and other elitist groups deciding on behalf of all

---

[106] You can read about this bias in Cirocco's essay, Chapter 3 of this book.

citizens.

Nevertheless, we profoundly believe that this bias is maintained by elites because it is the only way to keep total control and power. We state that the prejudice against freedom and the distrust of individual's capacities that the historical and political processes have created is fostered with the intent to preserve an omnipotent, interventionist and socialist state assuring the monopolistic management and ownership of power and of the commanding heights of the economy.

Finally, as Acevedo (2018) argues, people would not have to be worried about that all common Venezuelans will be shareholders of enterprises such as PDVSA. That does not matter, what matters is that it will be an entirely private and profitable enterprise. Furthermore, this proposal would not be a crazy thing, remember the Coca-Cola Company, Google, and many more companies have more shareholders than Venezuelans in the world.

How to desocialize enterprises in Venezuela?

We propose a privatization program –based upon the Austrian School's view to the best extent-. Rothbard (1992) shows the guidelines that we have adopted after considering the particular situation of Venezuela. He argues that "you cannot plan markets" (p.66) in a desocialization strategy and that the only thing you can do is "set people free so that they can interact and exchange, and thereby develop markets themselves" (p.66). He explains the impossibility to plan capital markets, as occurred in the failed attempts of some Western economists to develop stock exchanges. For these reasons, Rothbard (1992) explains "stock markets cannot be planned, …, you cannot have markets in titles to capital if there are still virtually no private owners of capital in existence" (p.66).

The history of Eastern European countries demonstrated that some privatization programs succeeded. For example, in the case of Georgia, after a Social-Democrat government and some attempts of privatization involving a lot of corruption, cronyism, and political influences, the new real pro-free market government started a privatization program headed by Bendukidze. I firmly believe, it is one of the most successful ones that my team has researched and studied during the writing of this proposal. Some other attempts of desocializing enterprises, with relative success, are not difficult to find in recent history. The privatization program headed by Lewandowski in Poland, with all its pros and cons, is another notorious example that when rulers let free markets rule, things go right.

There are other great experiences in privatization processes around the world, such as the United States, Canada, United Kingdom, and other countries (institutionally better than Venezuela) that were headed and managed by the government. But, people have to understand that Venezuela is very far away from the reality and context where those examples succeeded, for this our proposal is more close to the Eastern Europe countries that succeeded and were very close to the Austrian School view.

We argue that any privatization program for Venezuela should follow the four general recommendations that Rothbard (1992) provides about desocialization processes. 1) Drastic reduction in taxes, government expenditures, and government employment. 2) Returning property of the assets owned by the government to the original expropriated owners or their heirs, or granting shares to productive workers and peasants who had worked on these assets. 3) Honoring complete and secure property rights in the sense of providing complete freedom to transfer property. And 4) depriving the government the power to create new money.

Finally, and considering the current situation of

Venezuela[107], and in light of previous experiences of other countries undertaking similar privatization processes, some restrictions are included in our proposal, especially concerning points 2) and 3) of Rothbard's paper.

The Proposal

A draft of the Desocialization of Enterprises Law

This is an improved version of Acevedo (2018) that Acevedo, Cirocco, Faría and Lorca-Susino have developed to the paper "Desocialization of Enterprises: Empowering Venezuelans"

GENERALITIES

1. The scope of this law involves all State-Owned Enterprises (SOE) and State-Owned Assets (SOA).
2. The Beneficiaries (B) are all Venezuelans by birth and aged at least 18 years by the moment when the desocialization process takes place, residents or not in Venezuela. They will have to enroll in a private national or international financial institution of their preference, which will represent them in all the process.
3. The Desocialization Board (DB) will head the process.
    3.1 The DB will be formed as follow: one (1) representative per financial institution having at least 4% of the total Venezuelans enrolled in the process; one (1) representative per branch of the state: executive, judicial and legislative.
    3.2 All representatives have "voice" in the process, but just financial institutions' representatives have the

---

[107] One of widespread chronic corruption, at extreme levels, particular cultural characteristics, and the fact that the government effectively bought industries when they were nationalized

right to vote in a proportion defined by the number of Venezuelans they represent.

3.3 If a financial Institution does not represent 4% of the total Venezuelans enrolled in the process, it can delegate its representation functions to another institution.

3.4 All official and unofficial meetings of the DB will be broadcast live, recorded, and published, for transparency purposes.

3.5 All communications among the representatives will be considered public and will have to be recorded.

4. A Financial Rescue Fund (FRF) will be created as a fund managed by the DB to rescue some SOEs and pay liabilities. Funds will come from the process itself.

CLASSIFICATION

5. The DB will categorize the SOEs and SOAs into six groups:

5.1 Desocialization Group: those SOEs fulfilling the desocialization process requirements.

5.2 Rescuable Group: those SOEs that can reach the requirements of the Desocialization Group upon following this process.

5.3 Public Auction: those SOEs that this process could not rescue and SOAs not classified as Clearance Assets.

5.4 Clearance Assets: all SOAs totally depreciated or in junk conditions.

5.5 Expropriated Assets or Enterprises: all those enterprises and/or assets expropriated or nationalized against the will of their former owners.

5.6 Social Assets: all those assets related to social programs given to citizens with no full property.

PROCEDURE

6. The Present Value of all certified reserves of natural resources of each SOE and/or SOA will be included in their respective accountability.

7. For Social Assets: the DB will immediately transfer, along with the corresponding tenure, the full property of the asset to the citizens, without restrictions in the rights to sale, mortgage, build or rent. Citizens will not pay any fee for the property transfer process.

8. For Expropriated Assets or Enterprises: The DB, based upon consistent proofs, will proceed as follows

    8.1 If the governmental administration indemnified the former owner by paying a price lower than the real value of the asset at that moment, the DB will transfer the property back to the former owner. The former owner will return the surplus resulting from the difference between the current value and the received amount minus the difference between the value at the moment of the expropriation and the received amount; if that final difference is negative the DB will transfer the property immediately to the former owner with no fees, and the difference will be paid through the FRF.

    8.2 If the administration did not indemnify the former owner for the expropriated assets or enterprises, the DB will immediately transfer the property to their former owners. If the difference between the current and past value is negative, the DB will pay such difference through the FRF.

9. For Clearance Assets: the DB will open a public sale process, using a technological system based on blockchain, and sell these assets in batches. The system will be transparent, with full public access to information about prices, buyers, and sale conditions. Up to 25% of the raised funds will be destined to pay the

fees and other expenses associated with this process, including those related to the DB. The DB will deposit the rest of the funds in the FRF.

10. For Public Auction: the DB will auction each SOE and SOA through a technological system based on blockchain. The system will be transparent, with full public access to information about prices, buyers, and sale conditions. Up to 12.5% of the raised funds will be destined to pay the fees and other expenses associated with this process, including those related to the DB. The DB will deposit the rest of the funds in the FRF.

11. For the Rescuable and Desocialization Group: the DB will establish a desocialization date for each one and estimate liabilities for each company, even considering the human resources liabilities, and include them in the balance sheet up to the date of the property transfer.

DESOCIALIZATION PROCESS

12. For companies with Total Assets greater than Total Liabilities, by 30% or more: the DB will do a liabilities-equity swap, and transfer the property as follows:

   12.1   Through a liabilities-equity swap, each creditor, and employee, will obtain an exact amount in shares than the enterprise owes them.

   12.2   70% of the rest in identical parts to B, in the form of shares.

   12.3   The new Board of Directors of the enterprise, elected by the new shareholders through their legal representatives, will sell the remaining 30% of the equity with a premium no more than 30%, considering the initial restriction in point 16 below. Up to 10% of the raised funds will be destined to pay the fees and other administrative expenses associated with the process, including those related to the DB. The DB will deposit the rest of the funds in the FRF.

13. Companies with Total Assets less than Total Liabilities or Total Assets higher than Total Liabilities by less than 30%, even 0%:

13.1   The DB will determine if creditors can be proportionally paid, with no more than 30% of the available FRF at the moment, an amount sufficient to make Total Assets greater than Total Liabilities, by 30%. Procedure described in point 12 will be followed then.

13.2   If the DB determines that more than the 30% of the available FRF is required and that there is at least another SOE classified in the desocialization group, then the DB will have to wait up to the end of the process to analyze if this SOE can be rescued through the FRF. If, at the end of the process, this is the last SOE classified in the Rescuable Group and there are enough funds in the FRF, then the DB will use those funds required to accomplish the proportion of Total Assets and Liabilities described in point 13.1. If there are not enough funds in the FRF to accomplish the proportion of Total Assets to Total Liabilities described in point 13.1, and to rescue the last SOE classified as Rescuable, the DB will re-classify it into the Public Auction Group.

REMAINDER OF THE FINANCIAL RESCUE FUND

14. If the desocialization process ends and the FRF still has funds, the DB will proceed as follows

14.1   It will pay a desocialization process honoraria, in proportion to the represented B, to each financial institution. The grand total of this payment will be the 10% of the available funds.

105

14.2　　The rest of the funds will be distributed proportionally among all SOEs that followed point 12 up to the amount of the premium that point 12.3 establishes.

14.3　　If, after following point 14.2 the FRF still has funds, the DB will distribute them in equal parts to B.

FINAL CONSIDERATIONS

15. The property of all SOEs and SOAs that this desocialization program encompasses will include the property of the corresponding soil and subsoil.
16. For a term of 3 years, after the day of the official desocialization, neither any person nor any company can buy and/or hold more than 3% of the equity of any SEOs desocialized through point 12. Nevertheless, a person or institution can represent, through a legal power, more than 3% of the total equity.
17. There is no other limitation to foreigners than the one stated in this law.
18. New shareholders will be able to immediately transfer, back debts or sell their shares. Nevertheless, those shares given to B following point 12.2 will be non-negotiable and non-transferable for 3 years since the day that B receives them.
19. Immediately after the desocialization day of each enterprise, new owners and employees will privately bargain new rules and laws of their labor contract. They can establish new private deals and rules considering or not the national's labor legal frame.

Closing remarks

People could understand that our proposal deviates from an orthodoxal view of the free-market economy. This could be possible because we included some restrictions. For example, we restricted the freedom to sell shares, because we want to appease some critics that similar privatization programs had in other countries. In those countries "cheated citizens" sold –or changed- their shares, below their value –or for food or booze-, immediately after obtaining the stock, because they had no knowledge about it, after that everybody –even populist and socialist politicians- blamed the program and the free-market system.

On the other hand, this restriction is only for the actions that "B" will obtain through point 12.2. Which means that if a Venezuelan acquires shares because he is an employee and his labor benefits were paid with shares as the proposal explains, those shares can be immediately sold if he wants. Furthermore, this essay is just an advance of the proposal, which means that we are analyzing other possibilities, such as reducing or eliminating this restriction if think tanks, such as Econintech, and other institutions promote an educational and mass awareness campaign on the Capital Market.

Other relevant information about this restriction is that, although "B" cannot sell their shares, private financial institutions would represent and vote for them. This will allow taking advantage of the management and knowledge of true experts when the representatives select the new board of directors. That is the reason point 16 states that any person or institution can represent, voting for, more than 3% of the total assets.

About the purchase restriction of up to 3% of the equity, we impose it to avoid cartelization of the company in the early ages of the privatization; nevertheless, that percentage could change at the final stage of our research.

Nonetheless, restrictions would not be a significant problem for new shareholders. For example, if the old creditors, now new shareholders, own more than 3% of the equity, they have four ways to recover their money. First, they sell their shares in

107

batches, each batch up to a maximum of 3% of the company's equity to different buyers. Second, they sell under a "future contract" all their shares to whomever they want, they can grant to the buyer a legal-power to represent them. Third, they can actively participate in the company and, if they can, in the Board of Directors. Finally, they can give their voting right to another institution to represent them as investors of the company until they wish.

Venezuela requires a free-market economy and privatization is one of the fundamental pillars. However, it also needs other reforms, such as eliminate of labor laws that are incredibly rigid and expensive for companies, eliminate minimum wage because it is a distorting factor in a free economy, change the taxation system, privatize services, and of course eradicate, once and forever, the State's monopoly on money. All these proposals are in this book and/or will be in other projects in which we are still working in Econintech.

13. DESOCIALIZATION OF TAXES: A TAXATION SYSTEM PROPOSAL FOR VENEZUELA

By Rafael Acevedo, Luis Cirocco, & María Lorca-Susino

An important area to be reformed in Venezuela is taxation. At this moment, the country has one of the worst systems, inneficient and with high levels of bureaucracy that increase the cost of living, entrepreneuring and investing, and which represent a big stone on the road to prosperity. That is why my colleagues and partners of Econintech and I are in the process of developing a proposal we called Desocialization of Taxes. We try to allign it, as much as possible, with some relevant Rothbard's suggestions. Our hope is that some day Venezuela can be one of the countries with the simplest and lowest taxation in the world, based upon the fact that:
"The State is the only legal institution in society that acquires its revenue by the use of coercion, by using enough violence and threat of violence on its victims to ensure their paying the desired tribute" Rothbard (1981: p.66).

Privileges granted to particular economic elites and institutional arrays poorly limiting government's powers have been remarkable characteristics of Venezuela's socialist and mercantilist economy over the last century. Hence, Hayek's (1945) foresight cannot be more descriptive of the course Venezuela's recent history towards the establishment of the current tyrannical regime:

> In a planned society the law must legalize what to all intents and purposes remains arbitrary action. If the law says that such a board or authority may do what it pleases, anything that board or authority does is legal – but its actions

are certainly not subject to the Rule of Law. By giving the government unlimited powers the most arbitrary rule can be made legal; and in this way a democracy may set up the most complete despotism imaginable. (p.69)

Venezuela's institutions require profound reforms in order for the country to enter a virtuous circle of sustainable prosperity. Nevertheless, if individual liberties, rule of law and citizens' empowerment (as opposed to government's accumulation of power) are not crucial objectives of those new arrays, the country will not escape the vicious circle of backwardness in which it has remained for decades.

All edges –political, social, economic, judicial and administrative– are of paramount importance to achieve the golden goal of individual liberty. That is why, we propose several reforms to build a strong foundation, with the taxation system as one fundamental pillar to be re-structured, based upon Rothbard's (1992) statement: *"Taxes are parasitic and statist... invade and aggress against the rights of private property"* (p.68)

Venezuela's constitution contemplates three taxation layers: national, regional and municipal. However, the central government –national level– controls almost all layers of competencies, weakening the autonomy of the municipal governments, which turn out depending on the "good faith" or discipline of the central planners.

The central government rules, collects and manages the bulk of the most "profitable" taxes, such as those levied on income, company assets, excise, international trade, royalties on mining and oil extraction, and other special categories. In turn, municipalities (or counties) must wait for the central government to transfer funds or "download the required resources", always diluted throughout the bureaucratic network. Taxpayers, ultimately, do not enjoy the benefits of an efficient compensation in terms of high quality services, reason why Rothbard's statement "taxation is theft" gains notorious strength.

In light of the goal to promote economic freedom, our proposal defines a new taxation system for Venezuela abiding by the principles of creating a low and simple tax burden and eradicating government's independence of its taxpayers, necessary conditions to starve the government and firmly establish the rule of law and democracy (Faría, 2008).

The Proposal

A unique tax levying consumption

We propose the complete elimination of all other taxes and the implementation of a unique low tax managed directly by municipalities. We are working in the academic presentation of this proposal; nevertheless, we consider it very important to publish this first introductory version.

Economists mostly focus on incrementing public debt and expenditures. Many people are not aware that the great problem of those programs will be faced in the near future, when bills have to be paid. We argue that our proposals (a book with our complete "Rebuilding Venezuela" Plan will be published as soon as Econintech's financial resources allow it) better approach long-run growth beacuse they promote the private sector, boost investments, encourage people to entrepreneur, and diminish the state.

A logical implementation plan for this taxation reform is described below.

First Step. The immediate equal distribution, among all Venezuelans by birth, of the taxes that oil corporations are legally forced to pay. Every Venezuelan, aged at least 18 years, will have the right to obtain the corresponding fraction of these taxes and royalties so that governments become totally dependent, in fiscal terms, on its citizens.

Second Step. The elimination of all the other taxes, laws and rules of taxation. The current burden has to be minimized, which encompasses the elimination of taxes levying international trade, capital gains, inheritance, and others.

Third Step. The implementation of a new taxation law, which will create a unique low and non-progressive tax on consumption for individuals and enterprises, and a unique non-progressive tax on revenues just for enterprises. We estimate that a maximum consumption tax of 10% and a maximum revenue tax of 30% are enough to maintain the limited and non-interventionist state we expect.

The proposed system will respect municipalities' sovereignty. Each municipality will have the autonomy to impose a flat rate on consumption from 0% to 10%, policy with which we intend to promote competition among them to attract investments and people.

Fourth Step. The total amount collected via the consumption tax will be managed by the municipality, which will reserve 20% to be sent to the state government. The state government, in turn, will send 25% of the total received from its municipalities to the central or federal government, and will use the rest to cover its administrative functions and regional projects. For instance, Lara State has currently 9 municipalities; then, each one would send 20% of the collected funds (consumption tax) to the state government; Lara's governor would distribute such funds as mentioned: 25% to the central government, and the rest to pay administrative expenses and regional projects.

The revenue tax will be collected and managed by municipalities as well. Each one will send 30% to the state government and 30% to the central (federal) government.

Fifth Step. A particular consideration for natural disasters and other extraordinary contingencies. We propose that the central government impose and manage a temporary tax on consumption or on bank transactions in the case of a natural disaster or any other extraordinary catastrophe, but it will be limited as follow: i) the tax will not last more than 4 months in a year; ii) the rate will not be more than 3%; iii) the tax cannot be imposed more than two times in each presidential term.

Sixth Step. If the central government or any municipality needed to increase the rates above the maximum, impose a new tax or keep the temporary tax for more than 4 months, they would have to call for a referendum specifying rates and terms; people would vote to approve it or not. The central government and/or municipality will not be able to impose or increase a tax if people dissaprove it.

Seventh Step. It is neccesary to implement a law that limits public expenditures for the central government to a maximum of 25% of the GDP. For natural disasters and other catastrophes, such limit could be raised after the corresponding approval of the Parliament, just for a temporary period. None of the governments –central, regional or municipal– will be able to borrow from any national or international organization an amount representing more than twice the average of the last three years of fiscal incomes.

Eighth Step (*still in the process to be completely defined*). Municipal fiscal surpluses, if generated, will be accumulated in certified reserves, which will be deposited upon renowned international banks in the form of gold, silver or other kinds of sound money. A municipal reserve is much easier to audit than a country-level one. Each municipality, in addition, could distribute its reserves among different specific-purpose budgets: natural disasters, backing of loans received and backing of their own municipal currency or cryptocurrency. But every specific reserve will be tied to a very particular objective, and resources will be prohibited to be diverted for other purposes. For the particular case of reserves intended to back municipal currency issuing, the local government will be permitted to use them right after a previous decrease of their own money in circulation, with the intent to protect its purchasing power.

Closing Remarks

It is very likely that our proposals will not be implemented by the political "leaders" of Venezuela, since restricting government's power and dismantling their preferred mechanism to enslave society –populism– are never options for them, and since very sensitive aspects of the economy are re-defined –the monetary and fiscal arrays.

Nonetheless, since real freedom is our desire for Venezuela, we cannot offer a Keynesian approach like many of today's highly publicized views. Our aim is very far away from replacing a future of long-run prosperity and liberty by an illusory rebound of the economy resulting from applying central planning strategies one more time. At Econintech, we work for and promote the empowerment of individuals, liberty and sustainable growth. It is our conviction that this will only be possible if real free-market reforms are applied; hence, we think our proposal – in Rothbard's (1992) words- is *"unobtrusive and harmless as possible, and imitate the market as closely as it can"* (p.70).

14. DESOCIALIZING EDUCATION IN VENEZUELA

By Rafael Acevedo[108]

In October 2018, I wrote an OpEd on the Spanish blog of the Independent Institute title "The Free Education in Venezuela". I breifly described a proposal for the educational system in my country; indeed, it was the first "official" attempt to publicize Econintech's position about the reforms in the educational area. Currently, we are working on the formal –and academic- structure and presentation of this reform, which we think is very important as the economic reforms we promote. This is a more advanced and updated draft I wrote to this book. We do not need to make a lot of math and econometric models as Keynesians do because our proposal is a free market option and is worthless to waste time making models for something proved in many countries. In the best of my knowledge, this is the best way to give a high international quality educational service to Venezuelans.

I think about the great opportunity that was wasted in Venezuela and, the cause why our educational system is getting worse and worse each day. Socialists accustomed Venezuelan people to despise Venezuelan private education, at the point that if a person held a diploma from a private University, it was considered an indicator that he did not have the merits to hold a diploma of "good origin." Indeed, I also think that this belief was created for three reasons.

First, politicians monopolized education in Venezuela. As in all countries, the public education system has been used to create a

---

[108] I thank Professor Walter Block, from Loyola University in New Orleans and Senior Fellow of the Mises Institute, for his suggestions and comments on this essay.

bias that favors the Status Quo. Then, we have that socialist and mercantilist ideas, Marxism, Keynesianism, and the "culture of all for free" are the raw material in Venezuelan public institutions. Faría & Filardo (2015) explain better this situation. Nevertheless, for these reasons, for politicians –and the liberals of the Status Quo- is critical to keep it, as it has always been, public as much as possible.

Second, corruption and cronyism in the creation of new institutions. The State has always strongly intervened the educational private sector, imposing programs & syllabus, but also, it has obstructed the creation of new institutions through a highly bureaucratized process, then, this has promoted corruption and cronyism[109]. I remember that in Venezuela it was common to say that if you wanted to create a new high educational institute you had to give as a "gift" at least the 40% of the shares to the members of the National Committee of Universities (CNU for its initials in Spanish), otherwise you would not find the permits. This is why Venezuela had –maybe still has- its own "Czar(s) of the private education"[110].

The last reason is that, while the State regulates and intervenes the educational programs that private institutions offer and obstructs the creation of new institutions and degrees; also, it imposes a price control to these institutions. Therefore, you have a socialist cocktail of corruption, cronyism, and wrong incentives in this sector. Despite this situation, some private institutions have excellent management, and offer high-quality

---

[109] The tyrant Chávez eliminated any possibility of new private high educational institutes, but before this –even in pre-Chávez era- the corruption cases were publicly known about how educational entrepreneurs had to bribe the National Committee of Universities to obtain the governmental permits to create private Universities or Colleges and, even, offer new degrees. In a nutshell, a Private University, College, or Degree, started their activities with corruption and cronyism to obtain the permits.

[110] As a second generation of University professors, I have always had, since I was born, close relation with the high educational system and I meet people that lived in firsthand the process I am describing.

educational services, there are many cases of rectitude and outstanding administration in private higher education, for example (although I do not share the Keynesian and/or Marxist ideas that many of them impart) IESA, UCAB, Universidad Metropolitana, etc... Moreover, other regional private institutions that have hired professor emeritus from the public Universities with excellent curriculums, such as Universidad Yacambú, Universidad Fermín Toro, etc.

Nonetheless, Venezuelans still dream to have universities similar to American Universities[111]. They want their large campuses, impeccable streets, classrooms, laboratories, first rank professors, student services that never fail, and much more. Well, I dare to tell you that this would have been possible in Venezuela, but the "culture of all for free" literally destroyed that possibility. I am aware that I am touching a susceptible point, this is a non-healed scar, and a problem non-still understood, the educational system. Venezuelans not only want to access and have "the best education in the world" but also "FOR FREE."

Venezuelans -and I am aware that now many young Americans- should understand that when something is free, it does not mean its cost is zero. They should ask about where the resources are coming to give them those "free stuff" they want. Also, they have to remember that there is no endless source of funds in the world; even in the United States if all things are free, the sources will end in the future. A free educational system will end, in the long-run term, in mediocrity, and destruction of the possibility to consolidate an educational system with high international quality.

Considering this, I have drafted a proposal on how to desocialize the educational system in Venezuela. I have to remark that Econintech's team is still working on the final version of this proposal; nevertheless, I present its core in this

---

[111] When I wrote the article published in the Independent Institute's Spanish blog, I was talking about Auburn University because of I was attending an invitation in the Mises Institute.

essay. We follow as closest as we could, considering the reality of Venezuela, ideas of the Austrian School. We aim to let the private sector offers a high-quality service but giving the possibility to all Venezuelans to access to education through the voucher system. This proposal involves not only high education, but also the elementary, middle, high school, vocational, and technical education; of course, we also support the homeschooling system.

The Proposal

We understand that this proposal would be only possible under a real pro-free market regime, which involves the overthrown of the current tyranny and the possible social democracy that is waiting to start to rule Venezuela again. I have divided the proposal into the following steps.

Step 1: Municipalization and total autonomy

Elementary, Middle and High Schools administration will be transferred to counties, with their current budget. Universities will have total autonomy.

Step 2: Privatization process

Each institution through a committee will estimate how much owe to employees. They will estimate the value of the total assets and liabilities. In a public act, all employees, one representant of the county where the institution is addressed, one representant for the State government, and one representant for the Central Government, everybody will have the same proportional vote, and decide if the institution will be privatized with a for-profit or non-profit status.

For-Profit: the institution will be divided into shares as follow: i) an exact number of shares that represent the total debt for each employee. ii) if there is a remanent in the equity it will be offered to any person, other institution, or enterprise with no conditions, the funds collected will be invested in the institution.

118

The institution will be managed as for-profit as the rules and laws indicate.

Non-Profit: In this case, a Board of Trustees will be created. Nevertheless, the institution should have donors with the willingness to create a fund with the total amount of the Assets plus a fund with the total that the institution owes to employees. The institution will be managed as a non-profit as the rules and laws indicate.

Step 3: Tuition and Fees determination & Programs and Academic Degrees

The Board of Directors, elected by a Shareholders assembly, will determine the tuition and fees in the for-profit institutions. The non-profit will determine their tuition and fees through the Board of Trustees. There will not be any price controls.

Each institution can start any program or educational degree that it wants. Counties, State Governments, and Central Government could request the creation of some program, but the Board of Directors or the Board of Trustees of each institution will take the decision.

Step 4: The Educational Voucher System

Counties will finance the education in all its stages – elementary, middle, high, vocational, technical, and college- through the voucher system to those people that cannot access by themselves. Each county will obtain the funds to finance educational vouchers through the consumption and revenue tax[112]. Each county will determine the conditions to be eligible to the voucher system, the amount of each voucher, and will prioritize their residents.

People benefited with the educational voucher from their

---

[112] Acevedo, Cirocco, Faría & Lorca-Susino explain this system in Chapter 13 of this book.

county residence, can use it in any institution, of any county. Perhaps, some institutions will have tuition and fees higher than the voucher, nevertheless in a free market educational system will be other institutions that offer their services considering the voucher face value. If people want to enroll their children in an expensive school, they could use the voucher as part of the payment and have other social help such as a scholarship[113] or pay by himself.

Educational institutions will offer full and partial scholarships to their students, residents -or not- of the institution's county. These scholarships will be entirely -or partial- deducible of their taxes. Private enterprises can pay for the studies of other people, employees, or not, shareholders' relatives or not, in institutions in the same county -or other counties of the country- of the taxpayer, these payments will be entirely -or partial- deducible of their taxes.

Closing Remarks

This project will be possible if we can attract the attention of the population, and –perhaps, the most important- politicians want to implement it. The first is easy to achieve. The second is that in the short-run will not be possible. Venezuela is still in the hands of socialists, and it will be for a mid-term.

Our proposal try to show Venezuelans the path to have high international quality educational services. Besides, this does not mean, "Many people will be out of the possibility to access to education," this is a fake assumption Marxists, Keynesians, and "liberals of the Status Quo" want you to believe in order to keep their main source of bias and brainwashed. Venezuelans, and all people, that are hearing politicians promising "free education" – and many "free stuff"- should be aware that gratuity ever ends in misery; if you do not believe it... look at -or live in...- Venezuela!

---

[113] Promoted through tax incentives.

15. HEALTHCARE SYSTEM IN VENEZUELA: From Free & Social Right to an International Quality Service

By Rafael Acevedo & Luis C. Marchena

Marchena is a medical doctor that promotes the privatization of the health system in Venezuela. He is one of the founders and former Executive Director of the Movimiento Libertad Venezuela. Currently, he is living in Brazil and continues promoting the free market reforms. He is a Fellow of Econintech and follower of Austrian Economists like Mises, Hayek, and Rothbard. This proposal follows the idea that it is better to have an international quality service than a free social right that will end in a mediocre and miserable system. He promotes the implementation of vouchers to give people with temporal or permanent economic problems the access to the healthcare system. In a nutshell, this reform would be the end of the healthcare system problems in Venezuela if politicians understand that health is not a social right but a service that can be supplied with an international quality standard and help poor people to access it through the voucher system.

The healthcare system of Venezuela has the worst crisis in its history. Its decline started in the last 30 years. Nevertheless, its impoverishment was accelerated in the last 10 years. The increase in the maternal and infant mortality rate, newborn mortality, the absence of treatment for cancer patients and the closure of pediatric services in different regions of the country due to the lack of supplies, medicines, and personnel are proof of this. Official institutions do not publish clear and reliable health statistics for obvious reasons. So, how can Venezuelans have a quality Healthcare System? This essay aims to answer this question.

First, health is a very complex concept because it has

implications in different areas. According to the World Health Organization (WHO) is not only the absence of disease but a condition of complete physical, mental and social welfare. This condition will hardly be reached by any of us throughout our lives. Therefore, it is a definition that is not following reality. A more realistic explanation would be a subjective and individual perception of wellness, which varies depending upon some circumstances.

The half a million question is: Is the healthcare a right? The constitution of Venezuela establishes (article 83) that healthcare is a right and it is guaranteed for free by the State. Nonetheless, the reality is different. According to the WHO the "out of pocket expense" of Venezuelans[114], went from 50.6% in 1995 to 65.8% in 2013, is the highest in Latin America, so we could conclude that healthcare in Venezuela, despite it is guaranteed by the state, is of "facto" privatized, even in the network of public services. The significant problem is that you pay for a service but do not receive the quality that you could enjoy in other parts of the world.

Besides, the fact that healthcare is established as a right in the constitution does not make it one or does not make it immune to scarcity, and mediocrity. Healthcare systems are nothing more than a service, and as every service is an activity that tries to satisfy the needs of the clients, therefore, it can be considered an economic good, which is something for which you work and acquire, which may be a basic need (for example, food). These economic goods, use resources by definition "limited and scarce" and the fact of being considered as "free" or "right" do not make them endless. When we say that healthcare is a "free" right, we are saying that other people will have to pay for the medical bills of third parties.

The socialist view that healthcare is a right and free, incentives people to allocate their money and savings in other

---

[114] Defined as the proportion of the families' budget used to solve the different requirements of healthcare –healthcare expenses-.

things and not to self-cover their access to healthcare. The result of this lousy incentive is people facing the risks that a miserable healthcare system involves. On the other hand, the state has the alibi –and motivation- to intervene and impose controls in the healthcare service market, which diminish the quality of the service and promote no-orthodox medical practices in a kind of black market. In brief, the only loser is the people.

We want to be clear, and emphatic, with this. All human being have the right to receive medical assistance without impediment. Nonetheless, the service has to satisfy people's needs efficiently, and the only way you can assure this is through a private healthcare system and leaving the State off of it.

In Venezuela the problem of the healthcare system is structural. In other words, the problem is how it is conceived, an organization in which the State plays all roles, this is why moving from the current to an optimum stage, where we could enjoy an international quality service we have to apply radical free-market reforms.

Those radical free-market reforms will liberalize, privatize and de-bureaucratize the system. Luis Marchena with the support of Econintech has designed a 4 steps real free market reform which can be applied in a term no longer than 5 years. And we are introducing with this essay to let the world know that there are many real classic liberals, and libertarians, that are proposing what Venezuela really needs.

The Proposal

Step 1: Open the Market and Allow the Humanitarian Aid

The humanitarian aid is the first step to provide a solution in the short term to a problem that, as we have seen, is more complex. In parallel to international aid, the government[115] has

---

[115] We understand and are writing this essay with the clear understanding that the only way to apply this reform is a non-socialist

123

to open the healthcare market, which means the elimination of all governmental controls. However, the new government should apply three policies:

First, allowing private accreditation boards to guarantee the quality of the service. It is essential to eliminate all governmental permits that regulate the healthcare system. This would incentive providers –such as medical doctors, nurses, pharmacologists, private hospitals, etc...- to offer high-quality services for having a good reputation and consumers would be more insightful in the search for better services, quality already low cost.

Second, to eliminate all governmental restrictions on the production and sales of pharmaceutical products and medical equipment. This involves the complete elimination of regulatory agencies responsible for controlling medicines, vaccines, drugs and biological products. We propose this because in Venezuela these agencies serve to obstruct innovation and increase production costs. By doing so costs and prices would fall, and we would have a wider variety of products on the market, the market would also force manufacturers and sellers to offer more guarantees and better descriptions of their products to attract more consumers. Some people ask about who would ensure the quality of these products, the answer is that private accreditation boards which would try to give their "guarantee seal" just if the product is good enough to keep their credibility and confidence in the healthcare system. Again, consumers would win with this step.

Third, liberalize the healthcare market, including the insurance industry. This includes eliminating the legal restrictions imposed on insurance companies that do not allow to exclude some risks. Currently, in Venezuela, these companies have to cover a large number of non-insurable risks along with

---

government. Therefore, we hope –maybe- in the medium term a real free market movement can win the political war in our country. Otherwise, this proposal will serve only as other reference of real pro free market ideas never applied.

insurable risks, which significantly increases costs by benefiting irresponsible individuals and high-risk groups at the expense of responsible individuals and low-risk groups.

Liberalizing the insurance industry, providers could offer any type of contract, include or exclude any kind of risk and discriminate groups or individuals. This would incentive not only the prices fall, but the competition and therefore the quality of their offered services. Of course, consumers with some kind of risks could have their customized insurance this is a thing that in a free market economy you will enjoy because without doubts the market will try to cover that non-satisfied demand.

Step 2: Unification and Municipalization of the Healthcare System

The healthcare system in Venezuela is divided into different "sub-systems." There are health centers of the Ministry of Health, the social programs called "Barrio Adentro" that is managed by Cubans, and almost all ministries have their own health centers, i.e. workforce, military, education, etc... We propose to unify all these assistance centers and grant their administration to counties where they are.

We support the Municipalization because it is the only way the healthcare system can adopt organizational and technological structures more adapted to local realities. Also, the counties' management would be more flexible and adaptable to the following step. It is important to say that this does not mean that people non-resident of the county could not be served in any center, we are only talking about the management of the centers. However, this step would be temporal.

Step 3: Restructuring of the Boards of Directors and Self-Management of Health Centers

As in almost all state-owned companies, the healthcare system is managed by people that their positions were assigned for political reasons. These centers have a staff of doctors, nurses, bioanalysts, technicians, administrative and workers, who must choose the members of the board of directors of the healthcare center. We propose that they should have elections, but before an electoral committee should check if all candidates have the minimum requirements for the position.

Before the last step, the healthcare centers would have a self-management system where the patient covers a percentage of their medical expenses, and the municipality pays the remaining portion. The board of directors can manage the purchase of supplies, medicines and medical equipment, repairs, and infrastructure work with total autonomy with the incomes perceived. Many people argue against our proposal because how Venezuelans would pay for services, they have no money, at this moment is when we really do not know if who is asking is talking because only want to attack our proposal or do not know the real situation in Venezuela. Currently, if Venezuelans do not cover almost 90% of the supplies and medicines in any public hospital, they cannot be served because there are no supplies neither medicines in the healthcare system.

Step 4: Privatization

We propose a privatization program similar to the desocialization of enterprises law[116]. We state that employees will obtain part of their job benefits accumulated and not paid as shares. For example, the Hospital "Antonio María Pineda" has a value of $10,000,000[117] and is divided into 1 million shares, which means that the cost of each share would be $10 each.

A million shares would be distributed as follow: i) at least one share to each employee who will be reduced of their work benefits; ii) the rest of the stock will be offered in the national and international market, with no regulation.

---

[116] Acevedo introduces this proposal in the Chapter 12 of this book.
[117] This is a hypothetical example. We have not done any official and technical measure of the total value of that hospital.

It is important to remark that employees will have the first option to buy shares through their work benefits. For example, if a worker has accumulated work benefits about $500 the worker will have the freedom to decide how much of that in shares and in money he/she will perceive. Nevertheless, they always have at least one share. Once employees receive their shares, the rest would be sold, and from this moment, the healthcare centers will have a shareholders board, which will name a new Board of Directors. The center will begin to work as a private healthcare center, the employees would bargain with the center about their work benefits, and the government will allow them to have their own labor rules out or in the frame of the current labor laws.

Closing remarks

In this part we try to answer some of the most concurrent questions we have to hear when publicly talk about our proposal.

Why privatization? Almost everybody knows that the State is inefficient in the management of resources and administration of services, an example is that in Venezuela public hospitals have 90% of hospital beds throughout the country and attend 47% of hospitalizations, while hospitals and private clinics have the remaining 10% and cover 53% of admissions. Concerning the average time of hospitalization, in public hospitals, the average hospitalization is 18 days and in a private center is 4 days. Which is more efficient in the management of resources?

Can poor people access to the healthcare system with this scheme? The short answer is yes. Currently, citizens through taxes finance the health system expenses, but those resources are mismanaged. Bureaucracy takes a significant part of resources, the government directly fund the healthcare centers through the payment of salaries, purchase of supplies among other things, in economic terms, the state finances the offer. We have never been against helping poor people, but we are entirely against indirect subsidies like the current system. This is why we propose that the State finances the demand. Which means, the State will fund access to the healthcare system for the poorest through social vouchers.

What is a health voucher? It is a direct subsidy that the county gives to those people who lack the resources to access the healthcare system. With this health voucher, the beneficiary will have the freedom to choose which insurance company and what type of health insurance he will hire for himself and his family, and later decide when he needs it in which private medical center he will receive medical attention. These social vouchers are going to be financed by the taxes collected by the counties.

What happens with high-cost diseases? They may be financed through companies to hospitals and specialized institutions in the treatment of these in exchange for tax incentives, it is important to remember that after the opening of the market that we mentioned before, the cost of treating these types of diseases will decrease considerably.

Finally, this proposal is the path from a miserable healthcare system to an international quality healthcare service. But, How to apply it? There are many ways, including the use of the Blockchain system that provides solutions in this and many other areas eradicating the omnipresence and interventionism of the State.

16. PROBLEMS OF DISTRIBUTIVE JUSTICE IN VENEZUELA'S POST-SOCIALISM TRANSITION

By Alejandro Chafuén[118]

Alex is one relevant reference to the free market movement. He has dedicated his life and work to promote economic freedom. Chafuén is Managing Director, International of the Acton Institute. He was president and CEO of Atlas Network from 1991-2018 and is president and founder of the Hispanic American Center of Economic Research. Alex holds a Ph.D. from the International College in California. I had the honor to meet him during my Smith Fellowship when he was president of the Atlas Network. I can say, with no fear to be wrong, he is one of the most dedicated persons to support and encourage the fight for freedom in the world. In this article, Alex suggests to Venezuelans that will be on charge of the justice, once the tyranny is overthrown, to work on distributive justice, the creation of a committee of experts, and request support from institutions "with credibility in topics of justice and morality." Venezuela will need to follow his suggestions if during the transition we want to have an honest, impartial and credible judicial system.

Communism has been defined as an economic system based on state ownership of the means of production. Socialism is usually a gentler version of communism, leaving some means of production in private hands.

During the last century, communist and socialist leaders included workers among these "means of production," and thus restricted their right to emigrate and even their right to change jobs or careers. Until very recently in China there were also

---

[118] Translation by Joshua Gregor

heavy restrictions on moving to different regions of the country. For those from certain regions there are still restrictions on the use of state services.

Except in a number of cases of targeted individuals and political prisoners, twenty-first-century socialism, as in the case of Venezuela, has not reached that extreme. We can say that a transition from such socialism to a free society has begun when a continuous process of weakening of the state apparatus of coercion is evident in both the economic and political spheres. This process can begin in just one of these areas, but it only becomes real and, in a sense, irreversible when it involves both areas. In China and Vietnam, for instance, the change took place more in the economic than the political sphere.

Distributive Justice[119]

Problems of justice fall under (a) commutative justice (justice in transactions and contracts) and (b) distributive justice (what every participant should contribute to decisions that have a "common" cost, and how much each should receive from the "common pool").

The usual topic of justice in post-socialist transitions is the restitution of private property to its legitimate owners. Such restitution, though, seems a topic for commutative justice. If the confiscated property came under state control, however, part of the restitution should also be guided by principles of distributive justice[120].

Analysis of distributive justice began with Aristotle (384-322 BC) and gained traction with St. Thomas Aquinas (1225-1274). Aristotle noted that distributive justice "is manifested in

---

[119] I analyze the topic of distributive justice more broadly in Chafuén (1985)

[120] See Chafuén (2003). This paper, used as a basis for a presentation of a transition in Cuba, was written after ten years of the fall of the Berlin Wall and expands on some of the points presented here.

distributions of honor or money or the other things that fall to be divided among those who have a share in the constitution." In the Aristotelian view, justice in distribution is achieved when the distribution is made according to merit; private goods are not objects of distributive justice.

In the Summa theologiae, St. Thomas—in line with Aristotle's thought—concluded that there is an "order of that which belongs to the community in relation to each single person. This order is directed by distributive justice, which distributes common goods proportionately."

Who is responsible for maintaining distributive justice? St. Thomas notes that "the act of distributing the goods of the community belongs to none but those who exercise authority over those goods"[121] —that is, governors, bureaucrats, and all those responsible for the care and provision of some common good. Distributive justice is vested in other individuals only passively: "Distributive justice is also in the subjects to whom those goods are distributed in so far as they are contented by a just distribution. Moreover distribution of common goods is sometimes made not to the state but to the members of a family, and such distribution can be made by authority of a private individual." [122]

What is the manner of this distribution of common goods among citizens? St. Thomas here follows Aristotelian lines: such goods must be distributed proportionally. The scholastic authors who followed St. Thomas also continued in this Aristotelian-Thomistic line. Themes such as profit, salaries, and interest were taken up as topics of commutative justice. The scholastics concluded that it was not the government's task to determine salaries, profits, and interest. To analyze these, the scholastics proceeded in the same way as when they studied the prices of goods; these, they determined, should be established according to common market appraisal without fraud, coercion, or

---

[121] *Ibid.*
[122] *Ibid.*

monopoly.

Challenges for Distributive Justice in Transitions from Socialism

"Playing favorites" is a typical attitude of those who violate distributive justice. Some concrete manifestations of this are nepotism and cronyism. It is an injustice in the distribution of common goods when one party is preferred to another not by reason of relevant merit but for another undue cause.

An example would be the giving of part of the common goods to a friend or relative. "This vice cannot be committed except regarding those to whom the goods are common. If a republic's common goods are distributed, undue partiality can be committed toward citizens who are part of the republic." This judgment changes when common goods are not involved: "If, out of liberality, someone should distribute his personal goods among citizens or hold a banquet, and leave his enemy out, such may be a sin against charity but it is not the sin of undue partiality; for here it is not a distribution of common goods." [123]

Undue partiality is not only condemned as counterproductive for society but is also condemned on an ethical level: "Undue partiality is the destruction of the republic and a cause of great detriment to it and its citizens. Thus it is by its nature a mortal sin gravely damaging to the republic." [124]

Corruption

Corruption, which often goes hand in hand with undue partiality, is another violation of distributive justice. Moreover, as I have shown in other academic contexts, corruption has a high correlation with lack of free markets and free trade[125]. Corruption

---

[123] Pedro de Ledesma, *Suma de Moral* (Salamanca: A. Ramírez, 1614), p. 286.
[124] Pedro de Ledesma, *Suma de Moral,* p. 287.
[125] Chafuén & Guzmán (1997)

tends to decrease to the degree that economic freedom increases. High inflation, overregulation, and taxes are powerful incentives to corruption, especially in countries with high inequality. In these cases, high tax rates have always led to widespread tax evasion, justifying a large informal economy and undermining respect for the rule of law. However, I consider it impossible to give restitution to victims of inflation and unjust regulations. Compensating them would create further victims and distributive injustices.

Another strong incentive to corruption is differential exchange rates and official exchange rates that diverge from free-market rates. These are easy to evade, can enrich bureaucrats and their associates, and from the standpoint of natural law appear so artificial that those who violate their regulations feel justified in their attempts. A merchant who declares that he is exporting less than he really is could be violating rules and lying, but the foreigners who buy from him see nothing wrong when asked to pay the total value to a foreign account or a subsidiary owned by the merchant.

Application to the case of Venezuela

Problems of distributive justice that will arise in Venezuela's transition can be divided into two large groups: those having to do with restitution to victims and those having to do with punishment for the guilty. If we have learned anything from similar transitions up to the present day, it is that not all victims can receive restitution for damages. At the same time, not all the guilty can be punished.

In reference to victims, some damages and wrongs—such as confiscation of property with insufficient compensation—can be calculated more or less justly. It will not be simple, though. Someone from whom a piece of land, for example, was unjustly confiscated may receive it back with its productive capacity almost intact. On the other hand, if the state confiscated an industrial enterprise or a factory and let it fall to ruin, or did not maintain the machinery or keep it up to date, the previous owner may only receive a generator of loss in return. This happened in cases in Slovenia that I was able to study. In one case the survivors received forests that the socialists had confiscated but left almost intact. In another case, survivors received an industrial enterprise that had only continued to exist in the socialist period because of special prices and conditions given by the regime. When these were returned, the forest property retained its full value; the industry was no more than a machine for creating losses.

Because of these ironies of life, the forest's owner at her death left a bequest to fight for economic freedom and against socialism in Slovenia; I had the privilege of administering this bequest. Thousands of people, however, never received compensation for their small confiscated properties and homes. There are similar cases in Venezuela, and the outcome will depend on how well distributive justice is fulfilled.

Take the case of steel companies, such as *Sivensa* and *Sidetur*, confiscated by the Chávez regime with no compensation to their owners. It is difficult to calculate the value of this business when it was confiscated and before the socialist debacle, but some place it in the billions of dollars. If when transition comes the business is returned to its owners, as is proper, what will its value be if all the machinery is outdated and poorly maintained?

At times there is "mixed" culpability, whose solution is very difficult even for expert theologians and legal scholars. *Sidor*, created by the Venezuelan state, was later privatized by President Caldera in 1997 and then renationalized by the Chávez regime in 2008. Compensation of nearly $2 billion was paid. Among those compensated, though, the Ternium company was accused of paying bribes to the Venezuelan government during these transactions. Likewise the owner of Ternium, Techint, of the Italian-Argentine Rocca family, is embroiled in Odebrecht's corruption. Although I am not a lawyer, I am aware of all of these topics' complexity. Some may say that bribing a thief not to steal everything is excusable. Bribing a Nazi guard to escape from

Germany is not the same as offering a bribe to obtain privileges from the Nazi regime.

I know of another case in Venezuela in which the dictatorial regime tried to resort to legal finagling to confiscate a large country estate belonging to a family I am friends with. Government agents tried to go back to property titles from the colonial period (back to 1492!) to argue that the land should belong to the state. The family decided to put up a legal fight, and, as happens in such cases, there came an offer that the government would back down in exchange for an under-the-table payment. The family members got together and honorably decided that they would prefer to lose everything rather than become accomplices of evil. Many of my Venezuelan colleagues have confirmed that this was not an isolated case and that many property owners endured similar threats.

There is a great deal, however, that we will not be able to calculate and restore adequately. The damaged caused by shattered dreams, professional careers cut short, deteriorated health, families torn apart... In Latin American countries that fought against communist guerrillas and in which socialists or their sympathizers then came to power, "justice" granted large compensation to former subversives. Millions must receive recompense from the Venezuelan state for harm to civilians caused by the Chávez and Maduro governments. Once socialism falls, the new Venezuelan government will have resources coming from reactivation as well as the resources it can recover from the guilty. But it will never be enough, and unequal treatment of victims is something that can affect the post-transition period. Three decades have passed since the fall of the Berlin Wall, and these debates continue today in post-communist countries.

Those making transition plans urgently need to carry out a comparative analysis of similar experiences and see which victims should be favored. Some of the more realistic transition plans envision the privatization of much of Venezuela's petroleum production. Part of this source of resources, like others

135

that liberation could produce, should be structured so as to benefit the most easily identifiable victims. But given the need to achieve economic growth fairly quickly, it is certain that only part of the victims will be able to receive what is owed them.

Regarding the guilty who profited from the twenty-first-century socialist regime, again it will be difficult to punish everyone. A distinction will have to be made between those who established relationships with the regime in order to continue operating their companies and those who, at the other extreme, created fictitious companies or used their own companies for unjust and corrupt profit. Again, there will be a lot of gray area. Some businessmen have the privilege of selling their products in airports; some have privileges in the exchange and financial markets. If these businessmen are not punished, they should at the very least bear disproportionate moral responsibility for helping in the transition.

One possibility is to focus the corrective work of distributive justice on the most serious cases. One punishment should be to prohibit those with greatest guilt from occupying public posts and certain business posts for a period of time. A case that Venezuelans ought to study is how the Brazilian justice system took up the theme of corruption in Odebrecht and Petrobras.

My recommendation to those responsible for justice during the transition is (1) not to neglect themes of distributive justice, (2) to work immediately to create an assessment committee made up of people who are beyond reproach and who have successful experience in these cases, and (3) to lend support to institutions with credibility in topics of justice and morality. For this assessment committee, from the Americas I would invite experts from Brazil and Chile, and from the rest of the world I would include experts from most of the countries of Central and Eastern Europe that left communism. To create support for decisions regarding distributive justice, it would be imperative to gain the support of the Catholic episcopate, among others. Before being clouded by the populist and statist view of social justice, the non-socialist tradition of distributive justice took shape in the

Catholic Church. Bishops and committed laypeople from this tradition must be the ones who bring back true distributive justice and help to rebuild Venezuela, aiding those who need forgiveness and those who build a healthy consensus.

EPILOGUE

WILL JUAN GUAIDÓ GIVE VENEZUELA THE FREE MARKET IT NEEDS TO SUCCEED?
By Benjamin Powell & Rafael Acevedo

Benjamin Powel is the Director of the Free Market Institute and Professor of Economics in the Rawls School of Business at Texas Tech University. He is Senior Fellow in the Independent Institute and is the author –with Robert Lawson- of the book "Socialism Sucks: Two economists drink their way through the unfree world." Powell is the North American Editor of the Review of Austrian Economics. He has published more than 50 scholarly articles and policy studies. In late January 2019, Ben and I wrote this OpEd that The Independent Institute and the Daily Caller published in March 2019. We explain that it is not only enough getting rid of Maduro but the implementation of real Free Market reforms. Sadly, when I was finishing the edition of this book, the intentions of politicians seem to be the same, keep the big state and the state-ownership of the commanding heights of the economy. "Georgia went from having a socialist economic system to now being ranked the seventh most economically free country in the world." Then, Venezuela could be the Latin American Georgia but if Venezuelans want to achieve this, and long-run prosperity, they also should get rid of all Keynesians and socialists, I know I am doing a redundancy, that does not want to apply real free market reforms.

It's been 60 years since the Cuban revolution swept Fidel Castro into power, much to the delight of American elites. Will history now repeat itself in Venezuela?

It's a grim possibility. The political stalemate between Nicolás Maduro and his would-be successor, Juan Guaidó, conceals an unfortunate truth: that Guaidó—who has been recognized as interim president by the United States and some 50 other countries—is no free-market reformer.

Make no mistake: Venezuela desperately needs to rid itself of Maduro and his oppressive policies. But Guaidó and allied opposition leaders don't support the type of market reforms Venezuela needs.

High oil prices masked the economic ruin that Hugo Chávez's brand of "Bolivarian Socialism" was inflicting on the country for years. But since the collapse of oil prices, shortly after Chávez's death in 2013, the economy has been crumbling as Maduro, his hand-picked successor, continued his ruinous policies.

Almost 90 percent of Venezuelans now live in extreme poverty. There are shortages of food, medicine and other basics; people are going hungry. Maternal mortality has risen 65 percent and infant mortality 30 percent. Hyperinflation is skyrocketing out of control. Four million people, including one of the authors of this column, have fled the misery to look for a better life abroad.

Unfortunately, Guaidó and the allied political parties belonging to the Democratic Unity Roundtable—known as Mesa de la Unidad Democrática (MUD), or "Frente Amplio" (Broad Front)—were more united in their opposition to Maduro's leadership than to the failed socialist policies. In fact, Guaidó's political party is a member of the Socialist International and he and his allies would like to return to the type of "light socialism" Venezuela practiced before Chávez came to power in 1998.

They favor state-ownership of "strategic enterprises," keeping the bloated bureaucracy as it is, protecting national industries from foreign competition with subsidies, and command and control state intervention in the economy. In short, they want a return to democracy, but with the same big government economic meddling that pre-dates Chávez.

Although Venezuela was doing better in 1998 than it is now, its economy had been in a long period of decline prior to Chávez coming to power. In 1957, Venezuela's real GDP per capita was half of that in the United States. After its "social-democrat era" began in 1958 its economy stagnated, and by 1998, when Chávez began pursuing more hard-core socialist policies, incomes averaged only 15 percent of U.S. levels.

Instead of the failed interventionist policies favored by Guaidó and his supporters, Venezuela needs true market reforms: privatizing state-owned companies and assets, including the state-owned oil company (PDVSA); eliminating such corrupted institutions as the Bolivarian National Guard; reducing government personnel; giving administrative and budgetary autonomy to counties; replacing steeply progressive taxation with simple flat tax; eliminating international trade barriers, and opening the road to monetary freedom by dollarizing.

Venezuela would not be the first socialist country to make these type of radical market reforms. The Republic of Georgia embraced most of these same policies following the 2004 Rose Revolution. Georgia went from having a socialist economic system to now being ranked the seventh most economically free country in the world. The results were dramatic. The pro-market reforms increased Georgia's income per capita about 40 percent, lowered infant mortality by 30 percent, and increased employment by about 10 percent, all while not increasing inequality.

Getting rid of Maduro is a necessary but insufficient step towards getting Venezuela back on its feet. If Venezuela is going to get off "the road to serfdom" and back on a path towards prosperity, Guaidó will need to give voice to Venezuela's market-oriented opposition groups—such as Rumbo Libertad and Movimiento Libertad Venezuela—and embrace real reform. Otherwise, the long-suffering country may simply be trading its old socialist boss for a new one.

REFERENCES

Prologue

Palmer, Tom. (2013). Why Liberty? Atlas Economic Research Foundation and Students for Liberty.

1. How to Promote Prosperity in Venezuela:

Anderson, William L. "Economists for Price Controls?" 2001. June 11. Available at: Mises.org

Bishop, Tho. 2018. "In Socialist Venezuela the Poor Starve to Death While the Politically Powerful Feast." September 20; Available at: Mises.org

Block, Walter E. 1995. "Professor Modigliani on price controls: the baleful influence of the perfectly competitive model," International Journal of Social Economics, Vol. 22, No. 5, pp. 27-30; Available at: Mises.org

Block, Walter E. 1998. "Private Roads, Competition, Automobile Insurance and Price Controls," Competitiveness Review, Vol. 8, No. 1, pp. 55-64.

Gomez, Alan. 2018. "Venezuelan President Nicolás Maduro blasted for dining on 'Salt Bae' steak as his country starves." September 18; Available at: usatoday.com

Gwartney, James, Robert W. Lawson and Walter E. Block. 1996. Economic Freedom of the World, 1975-1995; Vancouver, B.C. Canada: the Fraser Institute. Available at: fraserinstitute.org

Konstantin, Anatole. 2017. A Brief History of Communism: The Rise and Fall of the Soviet Empire. Konstantin memoirs

Liu, Rebecca. 2016. "The Chicago Boys now and then." September 27; Available at: kingsreview.co.uk

McMaken, Ryan. 2017. "Why the Left Refuses to Talk About Venezuela." May 18; Available at: Mises.org

Von Mises, Ludwig. 2005. "Inflation and Price Control." May 27; Available at: Mises.org

Mitchell, Daniel J. 2018. "Capitalism: Why Chile Is So Much Richer than Venezuela." July, 24; Available at: Mises.org

Murphy, Robert P. 2018. "How Not to Address Rising Oil Prices: Lessons from Nixon's Price Controls." April 26; Available at: Mises.org

Niño, Jose. 2018 "John Oliver is Wrong About Venezuela — It's a Socialist Country." May 30; Available at: Mises.org

Opazo, Tania. 2016. "The Boys Who Got to Remake an Economy; They embraced free-market economics in America. Then Chile's dictator let them transform an entire society." January 12; Available at: slate.com

Plokhy, Serhii. 2015. The Last Empire: The Final Days of the Soviet Union. Basic Books

Rothbard, Murray N. 1993. "Price Controls Are Back!" The Free Market. Auburn, AL: The Ludwig von Mises Institute, June, pp. 1, 7-8.
Schuettinger, Robert L. 1979. Forty Centuries of Wage and Price Controls: How Not Fight Inflation. Green Hill Publisher.

The Economist. 1996. "Economic Freedom: Of Liberty and Prosperity." January 13; pp. 21-23.

Van Cott, Norman. 2002. "Direct from Chile." March 25; Available at: Mises.org

2.   The Genesis of Evil

Faría, H. and Filardo, L. (2015). *Venezuela: Without Liberals, There Is No Liberalism.* Econ Journal Watch 12(3). September 2015: 375-399.

Faría, H., González, J., Penzini, L.; Pérez, R., Zalzman, S. and Zerpa, J. (2005). *Measuring the Costs of Protection in Venezuela.* The International Business and Economics Research Journal.

Faría, H. y Montesinos, H. (2016). *The Critical Role of Economic Freedom in Venezuela's Predicament.* Economic Freedom of the World 2016 Annual Report. Chapter 4.

Mises, L. (1980). *La acción humana, un tratado de economía.* Unión Editorial. Cuarta Edición. Madrid.

3. Capitalism and Entrepreneurship: an Essay on Latinamerica

Acemoglu, Daron y James Robinson (2012) Why Nations Fail. New York: Radom House

Acs, Z. J., & D. B. Audretsch, (1988) "Innovation in Large and Small Firms", American Economic
Review, 78, 678–690.

Audretsch, David B., Max C. Keilbach, y Erik E. Lehmann (2006) Entrepreneurship and Economic Growth. London: Oxford University Press

Bauman, Zygmunt (2009) El Arte de la Vida. Madrid: Ediciones Paidos ibérica

Baumaol, William, Robert E. Litan, Carl J. Schramm (2006) New Haven: Yale University Press

Blanchflower, D. (2000) "Self-employment in OECD Countries", Labor Economics, 7, 471–505

De Soto, Hernando (1989) The Other Path: The Invisible Revolution in the Third World. London: I. B.
Tauris

De Soto, Hernando (2000) The Mystery of Capital: Why Capitalism Triumphs in the West and Fails Everywhere Else. New York: Basic Books.

Edquist, C. (1997) National Systems of Innovation: Technologies, Institutions and Organizations. London: Pinter Publishers.

Friedman, Thomas (2005) "The First Law of Petropolitics," Foreing Policy. Mayo/Junio :28-35

Prosperity & Liberty: What Venezuela Needs?

Gargarella, Roberto (2013) Latin America Constitutionalism, 1810-2010: The Engine Room of the Constitution. Oxford: Oxford University Press

Kaufman, Daniel & Shang-Jin Wei (1999) "Does 'Grease Money' Speed up the Wheels of Commerce?" Policy Research Working, Paper Series 2254. Cambridge, Mass: National Bureau of Economic Research

Linz, Juan J. (1993) "The Perils of Presidentialism," (124-129) in Larry Diamond & Marc F. Plattner (eds) The Global Resurgence of Democracy. Baltimore: Johns Hopkins University Press

Lucas, R. (1988) "On the Mechanisms of Economic Development", Journal of Monetary Economics, 22, 3–39.

Lundvall, B. A. (Ed.) (1992) National Systems of Innovations. London: Pinter.

Lundvall, B. A. (1999) "National Business Systems and National Systems of Innovation", International Studies of Business and Organization, 29, 60–77.

Mainwaring, S. y M. Sober Shugart (eds) (1997) Presidentialism and Democracy in Latin America. Cambridge: Cambridge University Press

Mankiw, Gregory (2017) Brief Principles of Macroeconomics. Cengage Learning

Morgenstern, S., J. Polga-Hecimovich, y S. Shair-Rosenfield (2013) "Tall, Grande, or Venti: Presidential Powers in the United States and Latin America," Journal of Politics in Latin America, 52: 37-70

Nelson, R. R. (Ed.). (1993) National Innovation Systems: A Comparative Analysis. New York: Oxford University Press

O'Toole, Gavin. 2018. Politics Latin America. New York (NY): Routledge

Parker, S. C. (2009) The Economics of Entrepreneurship. Cambridge: Cambridge University Press.

Schumpeter, Joseph (1911) Theory of Economic Development.

New Brunswick: Transaction Publishers.

Smith, Adam (1776) The Wealth of Nations. New York: Random House, Inc.

Solow, R. (1957) "Technical Progress and the Aggregate Production Function", Review of Economics and Statistics, 39, 312–320.

Stepahn, A. y Cindy Skach (1993) "Constitutional Framework and democratic Consolidation: Parliamentarianism versus Presidentialism," World Politics, 46 (1), Octubre 1-22

Romer, P. (1990) "Endogenous Technological Change", Journal of Political Economy, 98, 71–102.

van Praag, M. C. (2007) "What Is the Value of Entrepreneurship Research: A Review of Recent Research", Small Business Economics, 29, 351–382.

Wei, Shange Jin (2000) "Local Corruption and Global Capital Flows," Brookings Papers of Economic Activity, 2: 303-46

6. Poland: Stabilization and Reforms under Extraordinary Politics

Balcerowicz, Leszek, 1992, 'Leszek Balcerowicz Defends the Shock Therapy', 'Transition' No. 8, September.

Balcerowicz, Leszek, 1995, 'Socialism, Capitalism, Transformation', Central University Press, Budapest. 'Gazeta Wyborcza', 1991, 30 October.

Hartwell, Christopher, 2013, 'Institutional Barriers in Transition. Examining Performance and Divergence in Transition Economies', Palgrave Macmillan.

Kawalec, Stefan, 1989, 'Privatization of the Polish Economy', Communist Economies', Volume 1, Number 3, p. 241 – 256.

Lewandowski, Janusz and Jan Szomburg, 1989, 'Property Reform as a Basis for Social and Economic Reform', 'Communist Economies', Volume 1, Number 3, p. 257 – 268.

Prosperity & Liberty: What Venezuela Needs?

7. Hong Kong: The Ongoing Miracle

The World in figures: Hong Kong and United Kingdom, The Economist, November 21, 2012.

Milton Friedman, "The Hong Kong Experiment," Hoover Digest, No. 3, 1998.

Catherine Schenk, "Economic History of Hong Kong," EH.Net Encyclopedia, March 16, 2008.

Central Intelligence Agency, The World Factbook. Country Comparison: GDP per capita (PPP), 2012.

Kui-Wai Li, Economic Freedom: Lessons of Hong Kong, 2012, p. 53.

Heritage Foundation, Index of Economic Freedom, 2013.

The World Bank, Ease of Doing Business in Hong Kong SAR, China, 2014.

Hong Kong Special Administrative Region Government, Hong Kong: The Facts. Coming to Hong Kong, 2013.

United Nations Conference on Trade and Development, World Investment Report 2013, 2013, pp. xiv-xv.

Hong Kong Special Administrative Region Government, Hong Kong: The Facts. Financial Services, 2013.

Z/Yen Group, The Global Financial Centres Index 14, September 2013.

Deloitte Touche Toh- matsu Limited, Taxation and Investment in Hong Kong, 2013, p. 2.

8. New Zealand: How Freedom Works

Mitchell, Dan. (2016). The Decline of Economic Liberty During the Bush-Obama Years.

Gwartney, J., Lawson, R. & Hall, J. (2016). Economic Freedom of

The World 2016 Report. Fraser Institute

Mitchell, Dan. (2016). The Productive People in France Need a Frexit.

Mitchell, Dan. (2014). The Golden Rule of Spending Restraint.

10. A Socialist Democracy: ¿Is It Viable?

Acemoglu, Daron and Simon Johnson (2005) "Unbundling Institutions", *Journal of Political Economy,* 113 (5): 949-995

Acemoglu, Daron and James Robinson (2012) *Why Nations Fail* Crown Publishing Group

Clark, Gregory (2007) *A Farewell to Alms* Princeton University Press

Cirocco, Luis; Faría, Hugo; Daniel Morales and Carlos Navarro (2019) Economic Institutions Do Cause Growth. Working Paper

Faría, Hugo, and Hugo Montesinos (2018) On the Origins of Democracy. Working Paper

Faría, Hugo, Hugo Montesinos-Yufa, Daniel Morales and Carlos Navarro (2016) "Unbundling the roles of human capital and institutions in economic development", *European Journal of Political Economy* 45: 108-128

Finley, Moses (1973) *The Ancient Economy* University of California Press

Gwartney, James, Robert Lawson and Joshua Hall. 2014. *Economic Freedom of the World 2012 Annual Report*, Vancouver: Fraser Institute.

Harrington, James (1992) [1656] *The Commonwealth of Oceana and a System of Politics* J.G.A. Pocock (Cambridge Texts in the History of Political Thought)

Johnson, Paul (1999) "Laying Down the Law" Wall Street Journal p. A22, March 10th.

Pipes, Richard (1999) *Property and Freedom*, Vintage Books, New York

11. Why Venezuela Should Embrace Dollarization

Hanke, Steve. (2017a). On the currency Reform that Put Montenegro Center Stage. In Forbes.com

Hanke, Steve. (2016). Remembrances of a Currency Reformer: Some Notes and Sketches from the Field. Studies in Applied Economics. Johns Hopkins Institute for Applied Economics, Global Health, and Study Business Enterprise

Hanke, Steve. (2017b). On Venezuela's Tragic Meltdown. Studies in Applied Economics. Johns Hopkins Institute for Applied Economics, Global Health, and Study Business Enterprise

12. How To Desocialize Enterprises: A Privatization Program For Venezuela

Acevedo, Rafael. (2018). La Desnacionalización de las Empresas del Estado. Available at: Econintech.org

Faría, H., & Filardo, L. (2015). Venezuela: Without Liberals There Is No Liberalism. *Econ Journal Watch*, 12(3), pp 375-399.

Mises, L. (2008). Profit & Loss. Ludwig von Mises Institute. Auburn, Alabama.

Rothbard, M. (1992). How and How Not to Desocialize. *The Review of Austrian Economics*, 6(1), pp 65-77.

13. Desocialization of Taxes: a Taxation System Proposal For Venezuela

Faría H. (2008). Hugo Chávez Against the Backdrop of Venezuelan Economic and Political History. The Independent Review, v. XII, n. 4, Spring, pp. 519–535.

Hayek F. (1945). The Road to Serfdom. The Institute of Economic Affairs.

Rothbard, M. (1992). How and How Not to Desocialize. The

Review of Austrian Economics, 6(1), pp 65-77, pp 65-77.

Rothbard, M. (1981). The Myth of Neutral Taxation. The Cato Journal.

14. Desocializing Education in Venezuela

Faría, H., & Filardo, L. (2015). Venezuela: Without Liberals There Is No Liberalism. *Econ Journal Watch*, 12(3), pp 375-399.

16. Problems of Distributive Justice in Venezuela's Post-Socialism Transition

Chafuén, Alejandro. (1985). "Justicia Distributiva en la Escolástica Tardía" in the journal Estudios Públicos, 18, 1985. Available at: cepchile.cl

Chafuén, Alejandro. (2003). Out of Communism: An Ethical Road Map: The Dignity of the Human Person as the Foundation of the Transition from Communism. Available at: ascecuba.org

Chafuén, Alejandro & Guzmán, Eugenio. (1997). Estado y Corrupción. Centro de Estudios Públicos, Santiago, Chile.

www.econintech.org

OUR NAME IS THE FUSION OF THESE WORDS: ECONOMICS, ENTREPRENEURSHIP, INVESTMENT, INNOVATION, & TECHNOLOGY:

ECONINTECH

Our Mission:

Econintech is dedicated to promoting the ideas of the free market in the areas of economics, entrepreneurship, investment, innovation, and technology by creating awareness and educating society about these ideas that will allow countries to prosper.

What we do…:

Founded in 2015 in Venezuela and registered in 2019 in the United States. We are a classic liberal/libertarian think tank committed with education and research to promote freedom & entrepreneurship as the best way to fight against socialism. Since our foundation, just in Venezuela, we have had more than 3,000 attendees in more than 200 activities. Now in the US, we promote entrepreneurship, educational opportunities, and a real understanding of freedom in the immigrant population to improve their quality of life and opportunities to protect the real liberty and free market economy in the USA.

How can you help…:

All your collaborations are tax-deductible in the US to the full extent the laws allow. Contact us to let you know how your gift will strength our work: contacto@econintech.org

BOOKS IN SPANISH PUBLISHED BY ECONINTECH

If you want to know the causes and culprits of the economic disaster in Venezuela, you should read this book. Editors, Dr. Rafael Acevedo and Msc. Luis Cirocco, Founder-Directors of Econintech, pay homage to the Venezuelan free-market economist with the most extended trajectory in contemporary history, Dr. Hugo Faría. Professor Faría is a Venezuelan of high human, professional, and academic quality, who has dedicated his life and research to spread the importance of real economic freedom and to defend the rights of the individual. You can buy it in Amazon and on the website of the Editorial Círculo Rojo. Available in Spanish.

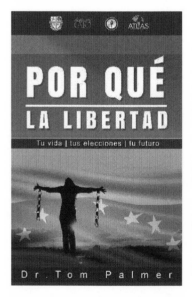

Thanks to the Atlas Network, Econintech could print and distribute among its attendees Dr. Palmer's book "Why Liberty." Through these events Econintech promotes the real libertarians and classical liberal ideals in Venezuela. Econintech's activities have benefited a high number of attendees with the lectures and presentation of this fantastic book. Econintech's Fellows-Scholars share the vision and principles of real liberty.

Made in the USA
Columbia, SC
16 May 2019